MYSTERIES
OF
MOUNT SHASTA

Home Of The Underground
Dwellers and Ancient Gods

Edited by Timothy Green Beckley
Inner Light Publications/Global Communications

Mysteries of Mount Shasta

Nonfiction – History/Metaphysics

Timothy Green Beckley, Editor/Publisher
Carol Ann Rodriguez, Publisher's Assistant
Editor in Chief, Sean Casteel
Cover Graphics, Tim Swartz
William Kern and John Anthony Miller, Special Consultants

ISBN
978-1-60611-002-7
1-60611-002-0

For Free Copies of the Conspiracy Journal and Bizarre Bazaár write:

Global Communications,
Box 753
New Brunswick, NJ 08903

(Please indicate title of this book and where it was obtained)

Or register online at www.ConspiracyJournal.com
For Translation and Reprint Rights Contact The Publisher At
MRUFO8@hotmail.com

MYSTERIES OF MT. SHASTA
Home Of The Underground Dwellers
And Ancient Gods

EDITED BY
TIMOTHY GREEN BECKLEY

Home of the Underground Dwellers and Ancient Gods

Contents

List of Illustrations

There Is No Place Like This Place
Introduction by Timothy Green Beckley

There are many sacred sites located throughout the world.

The Jews and Christians have their Jerusalem.

The Moslems have their Mecca.

New Agers flock to Sedona.

And everyone loves Mount Shasta.

For there is no place—certainly not in North America—that is more shrouded in mystery, so cloaked in enigma, to be found anywhere else in the world. With stories of the lost continent of Lemuria, to a landing base for UFOs, to the capital of the underworld known as Telos—this magical mountain attracts thousands each year. Some come just for the scenic beauty, others for a spiritual experience.

No one goes away empty handed!

Mount Shasta is listed with the U.S. Geological Survey as an "active volcano." A lot of volcanoes seem to attract the attention of UFOs. I know they do in Costa Rica, where I visited several years ago. They have also been seen and photographed coming out of one of the largest volcanoes in Mexico. Mount Shasta has its UFOs. They zoom around the place like there is no tomorrow. Just ask any of the witnesses who have seen unusual formations and singular craft in the sky just above the tree line. They have even been seen disappearing into the mountain itself.

I hope this book conveys various uplifting messages to those seeking a variety of experiences. For if nothing else, you should come to love one of the most beautiful creations on Earth—Mount Shasta.

Timothy Green Beckley
MRUFO@webtv.net
www.ConspiracyJournal.com

Fig. 1- Even Sodas Have Been Named After This Mysterious Mountain

History & Early Legends

THE MOUNT SHASTA PROJECT "REPOSITORY OF MYSTERY"

EARLY TALES OF OUR NATIVE TRIBES

THE *LOS ANGELES TIMES* PRINTS THE NEWS

THE WHITE MAN COMES TO SHASTA

Fig. 2- Early Woodcut of Mount Shasta - Garden of the Gods

Fig. 3- Early Map of the City of Mount Shasta

History And Early Legends

The Mount Shasta Project— Repository of Mystery

By Tim R. Swartz

*Tim Swartz is an Indiana native and Emmy Award-winning television producer/videographer. He is the author of a number of popular books, including **The Lost Journals of Nikola Tesla, Secret Black Projects, Evil Agenda of the Secret Government, Time Travel: A How-To Guide, Richard Shaver—Reality of the Inner Earth,** and his most recent, **Admiral Byrd's Secret Journey Beyond the Poles.***

As a photojournalist, Tim Swartz has traveled extensively and investigated paranormal phenomena and other unusual mysteries from such diverse locations as the Great Pyramid in Egypt to the Great Wall in China. He has worked with television networks such as PBS, ABC, NBC, CBS, CNN, ESPN, Thames-TV and the BBC.

His articles have been published in magazines such as "Mysteries," "FATE," "Strange," "Atlantis Rising," "UFO Universe," "Renaissance," and "Unsolved UFO Reports." Most recently, Tim has become the Associate Publisher for "Mysteries Magazine" and appears regularly as a special guest on Cosmic Horizons Radio (www.blogtalkradio.com).

In addition, Tim is the writer and editor of the Internet newsletter "Conspiracy Journal," a free, weekly email newsletter considered essential reading by paranormal researchers worldwide. View his website at: www.conspiracyjournal.com

One cannot help but be impressed when first seeing Mt. Shasta. It is a massive and imposing mountain that dominates the landscape for many miles around it. For many people, the mountain also seems to dominate their very inner being with a siren call that stretches out across invisible astral pathways drawing them in through time and space.

This psychic connection between man and mountain has existed as long as their have been people living in the area around the mountain. The major indigenous peoples of this area were the Shastans, Achumawi, Atsugewi,

Wintu, and Modoc. These peoples all lived within the mountain's influence. The Achumawi and Atsugewi called the mountain "Yet," the Wintu referred to it as "Behem Puyok," the Modoc identified Mt. Shasta as "Melaikshi," and the Shasta people called the mountain Withassa, or Wai-i-ki.

So much over the years has been written about the mountain that the College of the Siskiyous, located in Weed, California, has undertaken an important venture called *The Mount Shasta Project*. According to their website, head librarian Dennis Freeman recognized the importance of Mt. Shasta and its significance to academia. He began to gather material related to the mountain as part of the library's special collections.

The McConnell Foundation of Redding, California, provided the funding necessary to develop and publish an annotated bibliography of source material from the Mount Shasta Collection. The document that was developed through that project by William C. Miesse in 1993 chronicles hundreds of books, articles, manuscripts, and audio-visual materials pertaining to the great mountain. The majority of the works cited in the 289-page bibliography are contained in the College of the Siskiyous' Mt. Shasta Collection that is housed in the COS Library.

The Mount Shasta Collection is the largest repository of information and documents about Mount Shasta. It consists of thousands of books, articles, manuscripts, photographs, maps, prints, and audiovisual materials about the Mount Shasta volcano and surrounding area that can be accessed by visiting researchers, educators, and students.

Tales of the Native Americans

The Mount Shasta Collection has brought together an impressive number of Native American folklore concerning the mountain. The mountain has always been seen as a sacred place by Native American groups, and this relationship between mountain and man leads to a rich source of customs, myths, legends and folklore.

Roland Dixon published a tale in *The Journal of the American Folk-Lore* (Cambridge: Harvard University, 1908, p. 165) that relates the Achomawi and Atsugewi tribes' myth of the search for fire. The tale goes that after Hawk had been killed, and the flood had subsided, people found that all fires were put out all over the world. Nothing could be cooked, but for a time people did not trouble about it.

Then after a few days they began to talk about it, and sent Owl to Mount Shasta to look all over the world and see if he could find any trace of fire. Owl took a feather blanket and went. Lizard watched him go, and told the people how he was getting on. After a while, when Owl did not come back, people thought he was dead. But Lizard said, "Shh, I can still see him!" Owl got to the top at last, very tired, and wet with sweat. Lizard saw him look all about. He looked west twice, and there saw smoke coming from a sweat-house. After a while Owl came down from the mountain, and, coming back, told people what he had seen.

Next morning all got ready and went off to the west, to where the smoke had been seen. Every one had a cedar-bark torch. Dog had some punk hidden in his ear. Late in the evening they arrived at the house, and asked to be allowed to warm their hands. Dog held his ear down, and fire caught in the punk. Then every one thrust their torches into the fire, and ran.

The people in the house were angry, and struck at them as they ran off. Coyote's fire gave out first, then another's and another's, until finally all were out except that which Dog had in his ears. The people who owned fire had made it rain, and this put out the people's torches. No one knew that Dog had fire.

They got home and were much troubled, for they thought the fire had all been lost. Dog was laughing, and said, "I am sweating." Coyote got angry at this, and said, "Hit him! Knock him out!" Then Dog said to Fox, "Look in my ear." When he did so, he saw the fire. He took out the punk, made fire from it, and so people got fire again.

Also from Dixon in the volume 23, number 87 issue of *The Journal of American Folk-lore*, is the Shasta Tribe's story of the Coyote and the Flood. Coyote was traveling about. There was an evil being in the water. Coyote carried his arrows. Now, the evil being rose up out of the water, and said, "There is no wood." Then the water rose up toward Coyote, it covered him up, Coyote was covered by the water. Then the water went down, dried off, and Coyote shot the evil being.

Now, Coyote ran away, and the water followed after him. He ran up on Mount Shasta, ran up to the top of the mountain. The water was very deep. Coyote made a fire, for there only was any ground left above the water. Grizzly-Bear swam thither, deer swam thither, Black-Bear swam thither, Elk swam thither, and Gray-Squirrel, and Jack-Rabbit, and Ground-Squirrel, and Badger, and Porcupine, and Coon, and Wild-Cat, and Fisher, and Wolf, and Mountain-Lion. Then there was no more water. It was swampy all about. People scattered everywhere.

In 1873 Joaquin Miller published his groundbreaking book *Life Amongst the Modocs: Unwritten History*. Based on his years among the mining towns and Indian camps of northernmost California during the tumultuous 1850s, Miller wrote about a time when he felt he had completely embraced the Native American lifestyle.

Miller said that the Indian's life to an active mind was monotonous. "We rode, we fished, we hunted, and hunted, and fished, and rode, and that was nearly all we could do by day."

At night, when no wars or excitement of any kind stirred the village, they would gather in the chief's or other great bark lodges around the fires, and tell and listen to stories. The Native Americans said that the Great Spirit made Mt. Shasta first of all. He first pushed down snow and ice from the skies through a hole which he made in the blue heavens by turning a stone round and round, till he made this great mountain, then he stepped out of the clouds on to the mountain top, and descended and planted the trees all around by putting his finger on the ground.

The sun melted the snow, and the water ran down and nurtured the trees and made the rivers. After that he made the fish for the rivers out of the small end of his staff. He made the birds by blowing some leaves which he took up from the ground among the trees. After that he made the beasts out of the remainder of his stick, but made the grizzly bear out of the big end, and made him master over all the others.

The Great Spirit made the grizzly so strong that he feared him himself, and would have to go up on the top of the mountain out of sight of the forest to sleep at night, lest the grizzly should assail him in his sleep. Afterwards, the Great Spirit wishing to remain on Earth, and make the sea and some more land, he converted Mt. Shasta by a great deal of labor into a wigwam, and built a fire in the center of it and made it a pleasant home.

After that his family came down, and they all have lived in the mountain ever since. They say that before the white man came they could see the fire ascending from the mountain by night and the smoke by day, every time they chose to look in that direction.

One late and severe spring-time many thousand snows ago, there was a great storm about the summit of Shasta, and that the Great Spirit sent his youngest and fairest daughter, of whom he was very fond, up to the hole in the top, bidding her speak to the storm that came up from the sea, and tell it to be more gentle or it would blow the mountain over. He bade her do this hastily, and not put her head out, lest the wind would catch her in the hair and blow her away. He told her she should only thrust out her long red arm and make a sign, and then speak to the storm without.

The child hastened to the top, and did as she was bid, and was about to return, but having never yet seen the ocean, where the wind was born and made his home, when it was white with the storm, she stopped, turned, and put her head out to look that way, when lo, the storm caught in her long red hair, and blew her out and away down and down the mountain side. Here she could not fix her feet in the hard, smooth ice and snow, and so slid on and on down to the dark belt of firs below the snow rim.

Now, the grizzly bears possessed all the wood and all the land even down to the sea at that time, and were very numerous and very powerful. They were not exactly beasts then, although they were covered with hair, lived in the caves, and had sharp claws; but they walked on two legs, and talked, and used clubs to fight with, instead of their teeth and claws as they do now.

At this time, there was a family of grizzlies living close up to the snow. The mother had lately brought forth, and the father was out in quest of food for the young, when, as he returned with his club on his shoulder and a young elk in his left hand, he saw this little child, red like fire, hid under a fir bush, with her long hair trailing in the snow, and shivering with fright and cold. Not knowing what to make of her, he took her to the old mother, who was very learned in all things, and asked her what this fair and frail thing was that he had found shivering under a fir-bush in the snow. The old mother Grizzly, who had things pretty much her own way, bade him leave the child with her, but never mention it to any one, and she would share her breast with her, and bring her up with the other children, and maybe some great good would come of it.

The old mother reared her as she promised to do, and the old hairy father went out every day with his club on his shoulder to get food for his family till they were all grown up, and able to do for themselves. "Now," said the old mother Grizzly to the old father Grizzly, as he stood his club by the door and sat down one day, "our oldest son is quite grown up, and must have a wife. Now, who shall it be but the little red creature you found in the snow under the black fir-bush." So the old grizzly father kissed her, said she was very wise, then took up his club on his shoulder, and went out and killed some meat for the marriage feast.

They married, and were very happy, and many children were born to them. But, being part of the Great Spirit and part of the grizzly bear, these children did not exactly resemble either of their parents, but partook somewhat of the nature and likeness of both. Thus was the red man created; for these children were the first Indians.

All the other grizzlies throughout the black forests, even down to the sea, were very proud and very kind, and met together, and, with their united strength, built for the lovely little red princess a wigwam close to that of her father, the Great Spirit. This is what is now called "Little Mount Shasta."

After many years, the old mother Grizzly felt that she soon must die; and, fearing that she had done wrong in detaining the child of the Great Spirit, she could not rest till she had seen him and restored him his long-lost treasure, and asked his forgiveness. With this object in view, she gathered together all the grizzlies at the new and magnificent lodge built for the Princess and her children, and then sent her eldest grandson to the summit of Mount Shasta, in a cloud, to speak to the Great Spirit and tell him where he could find his long-lost daughter.

When the Great Spirit heard this he was so glad that he ran down the mountainside on the south so fast and strong that the snow was melted off in places, and the tokens of his steps remain to this day. The grizzlies went out to meet him by thousands; and as he approached they stood apart in two great lines, with their clubs under their arms, and so opened a lane by which he passed in great state to the lodge where his daughter sat with her children.

But when he saw the children, and learned how the grizzlies that he had created had betrayed him into the creation of a new race, he was very wroth, and frowned on the old mother Grizzly till she died on the spot. At this the grizzlies all set up a dreadful howl; but he took his daughter on his shoulder, and turning to all the grizzlies, bade them hold their tongues, get down on their hands and knees, and so remain till he returned. They did as they were bid, and he closed the door of the lodge after him, drove all the children out into the world, passed out and up the mountain, and never returned to the timber any more.

So the grizzlies could not rise up any more, or use their clubs, but have ever since had to go on all-fours, much like other beasts, except when they have to fight for their lives, when the Great Spirit permits them to stand up and fight with their fists like men. That is why the Native Americans about Mt. Shasta will never kill or interfere in any way with a grizzly. Whenever one of their number is killed by one of these kings of the forest, he is burned on the spot, and all who pass that way for years cast a stone on the place till a great pile is thrown up. Fortunately, however, grizzlies are not plentiful about the mountain.

In proof of the truth of the story that the grizzly once walked and stood erect, and was much like a man, they show that he has scarcely any tail, and that his arms are a great deal shorter than his legs, and that they are more like a man than any other animal.

The Name "Shasta"

An interesting section of the *Mount Shasta Project* discusses the various possibilities on where Mt. Shasta received its unique name. Those who first visit the Mt. Shasta region often inquire where the name "Shasta" came from. The four most common reasons offered are:

1. The mountain is named after a very famous local Indian.

2. It is named after a local Indian tribe.

3. It comes from the Indian word Tsasdi, meaning "three" and refers to the   triple-peaked mountain.

4. The Russians who settled at Bodega could see it from the Coast Range. They called it Tchastal or "the white and pure mountain."

William Miesse, author of *Mount Shasta: An Annotated Bibliography*, has extensively researched this issue. According to Miesse, Peter Skene Ogden (in his 1826-27 journal) refers to a mountain, a tribe, and a river as "Sastice" "Castice" "Sistise" and "Sasty."

Based on his description, we know the mountain he was referring to was actually what is now known as Mt. McLoughlin in Southern Oregon. The Sastise River is now called the Rogue (some Indians in the area referred to themselves as "Kqwu'-sta"). It is also believed that the Wilkes Expedition (1838-42) mistakenly transposed Ogden's Sastise to the mountain that is today called Shasta.

By the time of the Gold Rush (1849) many maps of the area showed the mountain with names such as "Shasty," "Shaste," and "Sasty." Also, between 1842 and 1850 a number of journals and maps listed the mountain as Saste, Sasty, Shaste, Shasty, Shatasla, Sastise, Castice, and Sistise. The modern spelling (Shasta) did not appear until 1850 when the name was first chosen for Shasta County by the California State Legislature.

Local legends state that the mountain was named after a great king who traveled to the area from his land located somewhere across the western ocean. The king was named Shasta, and along with a small group of his people, settled around the mountain because its snow-capped peaks reminded them of their home.

When the Native American tribes began to settle into the area, they found it already occupied by the Shasta people, who were described as being shorter than the Native Americans and having dark hair and brown skin. The Shasta people fought to keep the invaders from their mountain, but the Native Americans were far more numerous and eventually drove the Shasta people away.

Some say the survivors left by canoe to find their original homeland, but despaired of ever finding it as their legends stated that it had been covered over by the ocean. The old tales of King Shasta and his lost people were kept alive by the Native Americans who from then on called the mountain "Shasta."

Other Legends of the Mountain

The *Mount Shasta Project* admits that by far the most popular example of Mt. Shasta lore is the spiritual connection with the alleged survivors of the mythical land of Lemuria. According to William Miesse, "In the mid-19th Century paleontologists coined the term 'Lemuria' to describe a hypothetical continent, bridging the Indian Ocean, which would have explained the migration of lemurs from Madagascar to India. Lemuria was a continent which submerged and was no longer to be seen."

The connection between Mt. Shasta and Lemuria came in 1905 with the publication of Frederick S. Oliver's book *A Dweller on Two Planets*. Michael Zanger writes in his book *Mt. Shasta: History, Legend and Lore*, that teenager Frederick Spencer Oliver, who was born in Washington D.C. in 1866 and came to Yreka, California, with his parents when he was two years old, was helping mark the boundaries of his family's mining claim during the summer of 1883. As the young man drove wooden stakes along a survey line, he jotted down the number and location of each stake in a notebook. At one point, as he took up his pencil to enter the information, his hand began to write uncontrollably.

Terrified, he ran two miles home to his parents. His mother fetched more writing paper, and Frederick continued to write until the strange force left his hand and arm. Over the next three years his hand would periodically be seized with the unusual force, and he would slowly write one or more pages. He finished the manuscript in 1895 and *A Dweller on Two Planets* became one of the first American occult classics and was followed by an equally popular sequel, *An Earth Dweller's Return*.

In describing his writing, Oliver claimed that he had been chosen as "amanuensis," or secretary, to the Lemurian spirit Phylos, and that the book had been dictated to him through "automatic writing." Oliver claimed that Phylos, who lived several previous incarnations on Atlantis, took him to the mysterious temples and dwelling places of a mystic brotherhood within Mt. Shasta.

A Dweller on Two Planets was undoubtedly ahead of its time as Oliver goes into great detail about antigravity, mass transit, the use of "dark-side" energy (which today would be called "zero point energy"), and devices such as voice-operated typewriters. The cigar-shaped, highly maneuverable Atlantean flying machines, or vailx, have an eerie resemblance to 20th Century UFO reports.

The Mt. Shasta legends of a city inside of the mountain are part of a long tradition of such legends from around the world. Oliver's book can be viewed as an attempt to bring ancient myths of hidden worlds within the Earth into the modern, technological age, (albeit the modern age of the late 19th century).

Fig. 4- Mount Shasta Collection Library

Home of the Underground Dwellers and Ancient Gods

A Dweller on Two Planets is still in print today, and has become the fountainhead of an entire genre of Mt. Shasta literature. Spencer Lewis, Eugene Thomas, Guy Ballard, Nola Van Valer, Earlyne Cheney, Elizabeth Clare Prophet, and a dozen other New Age believers have borrowed extensively from it. Dozens of groups, cults, churches, mystery schools and other spiritual seekers can also trace their roots back to the book.

For anyone interested in Mount Shasta, its fascinating history along with the myths and legends that surround the mysterious mountain, the Mount Shasta Collection offers an almost endless source of information. This is sure to delight anyone who is eager to learn more about the mountain that has become a spiritual Mecca to those whose souls yearn to connect with the mysteries of life, creation, and the universe.

To learn more about the Mount Shasta Collection, visit their website at: http://www.siskiyous.edu/library/shasta/

Fig. 5- Climbers on the Extreme Summit of Mount Shasta

Fig. 6- Mount Shasta Natives

**Fig. 7- Edward Kern (1823-1863), Forest Camp at Shastl Peak
Showing Natives Camped in the Shadow of the Mount**

History and Early Legends

Myths and Tales of Our Native Tribes

By Joaquin Miller

Called the "Poet of the Sierras" and the "Byron of the Rockies," Joaquin Miller (1837-1913) was also termed a "poseur" and a "farce" during his careers as a 19th century lawyer, judge, pony express rider, newspaperman, teacher, cook, miner conservationist and poet. Miller, though, always explained: "I am not a liar. I simply exaggerate the truth."

At an early point in his varied career, Miller came to live among the Indians on Mount Shasta and is even said to have fathered a child there with a Native-American woman. The child's name was Cali-Shasta, which means "Lily of Shasta." Miller hoped to create an independent utopian community on the mountain, to be called the "Shasta Republic." Like many of his elusive dreams, however, it never came to fruition. One can nevertheless read this account of some of the local Indian legends and take them however you choose.

To the Indian, a legend was simply an oral way in which to record their history. In olden days, they had no paper on which to record that which had taken place among them throughout their history, so instead, they told their tales orally, over the campfires, and each and every Indian was required to learn the tales in all their accuracy. The storyteller, or official historian of the tribe, was required to repeat these legends verbatim; to deviate in any form was forbidden. The legends had to be related word for word as learned from the elders, and their authenticity was never doubted.

The Indians have a term which they use in reference to the telling of their legends, "Yease Nicopesh." The interpretation means simply, "The truth and nothing but the truth."

Joaquin Miller, a noted writer of the late 1800s, lived for a period of time with the Indians of the Mt. Shasta region, and he recorded several of their legends. One particular legend was quite interesting in that it told how the mountain was created and of the creation of the Indian race. In Joaquin's own pen, the following tale was recorded:

"The Indians say the Great Spirit made this mountain first of all. He first pushed down snow and ice from the skies through a hole which he made in the blue heavens by turning a stone around and around till he made this great mountain, then he stepped down out of the clouds on to the mountaintop and descended and planted the trees all around by putting his finger on the ground. The sun melted the snow and the water ran down and nurtured the trees and made the rivers. After that he made the fish for the rivers out of the small end of his staff. He made the birds by blowing some leaves which he took from the ground among the trees. After he made the beasts out of the remainder of his stick, but made the grizzly bear out of the end, and made him master over all the others. He made the grizzly so strong that he feared him himself and would have to go up on top of the mountain out of sight of the forest to sleep at night. Lest the grizzly, who was, as will be seen, much more strong and cunning than now, should assail him in his sleep. Afterwards, the Great Spirit, wishing to remain on earth, and make the sea and some more land, converted Mt. Shasta by a great deal of labor into a wigwam, and built a fire in the center of it and made it a pleasant home. After that, his family came down, and they all have lived in the mountain ever since. They say that before the white man came they could see the fire ascending from the mountain at night and the smoke by day, every time they chose to look in that direction.

"The old Indians tell us that a storyteller is held in great repute; but he is not permitted to lie or romance under any circumstances. All he says must bear the stamp of truth or he is disgraced forever. Telling stories, their history, traditions, travels and giving and receiving lessons in geography are their chief diversions around the their camp and wigwam fires; except the popular and never-exhausted subject of their wars with the white men.

"There is a story published that these Indians will not ascend Mt. Shasta for fear of the Great Spirit there. This is only partly true. They will not ascend the mountain above the timberline under any circumstances; but it is not fear of either good or evil that restrains them. It is their profound veneration of the Great Spirit, the Great Spirit who dwells in this mountain with his people as a tent.

"One late and severe springtime many thousand snows ago, there was a great storm about the summit of Shasta, and the Great Spirit sent his youngest and fairest daughter, of whom he was very fond, up to the hole in the top, bidding her speak to the storm that came up from the sea, and tell it to be more gentle or it would blow the mountain over. He bade her do this hastily, and not put her head out, lest the wind would catch her in the hair and blow her away. He told her she should only thrust out her long red arm and make a sign, and then speak to the storm without.

"The child hastened to the top, and did as she was bid, and was about to return, but having never yet seen the ocean, where the wind was born and made his home, when it was white with storm, she stopped, turned and put her head out to look that way, when lo, the storm caught in her long hair and blew her out and away down and down the mountainside. Here she could not fix her feet in the hard, smooth ice and snow, and so slid on and on down to the dark belt of firs below the snow rim.

"Now, the grizzly bears possessed all the wood and all the land, even the sea at that time, and were very numerous and very powerful. They were not exactly beasts then, although they were covered with hair and lived in caves, and had sharp claws; but walked on two legs, and talked and used clubs to fight with, instead of their teeth and claws as they do now.

"At the time, there was a family of grizzlies living close up to the snow. The mother had lately brought forth and the father was out in quest of food for the young, when as he returned with his club on his shoulder and a young elk in his left hand, he saw this little child, red like fire, hid under a fir-bush, with her long hair trailing in the snow, and shivering with fright and cold. Not knowing what to make of her, he took her to the old mother, who was very learned in all things, and asked her what this fair and frail thing was that he found shivering under a fir-bush in the snow. The old mother grizzly, who had things pretty much her own way, bade him leave the child with her, but never mentioned it to anyone, and she would share her breast with her and bring her up with the other children, and maybe some great good would come of it.

"The old mother reared her as she promised to do, and the old hairy father went out every day with his club on his shoulder to get food for his family till they were all grown and able to do for themselves.

"'Now,' said the old mother grizzly to the old father, as he stood his club by the door and sat down one day, 'our oldest son is quite grown up, and must have a wife. Now, who shall it be but the little red creature you found in the snow under the black fir-bush.' So the old grizzly father kissed her, said she was very wise, then took up his club on his shoulder and went out and killed some meat for the marriage feast.

"They married and were very happy, and many children were born to them. But, being part of the Great Spirit and part grizzly bear, these children did not exactly resemble either of their parents, but partook somewhat of the likeness of both. Thus was the red man created; for these children were the first Indians.

"All the other grizzlies throughout the black forests, even down to the sea, were very proud and very kind, and met together, and with their united strength, built the lovely red princess a wigwam close to that of her father, the Great Spirit. This is now called 'Little Mount Shasta' (Black Butte).

"After many years, the old mother grizzly felt that she soon must die; and fearing that she had done wrong in detaining the child of the Great Spirit, she could not rest until she had seen him and restored him his long lost treasure, and asked his forgiveness.

"With this object in view, she gathered together all the grizzlies at the new magnificent lodge built for the princess and her children, and then sent her eldest grandson to the summit of Mt. Shasta, in a cloud, to speak to the Great Spirit and tell him where he could find his long lost daughter.

"When the Great Spirit heard this, he was so glad that he ran down the mountainside on the south so fast and strong that the snow melted off in places, and the tokens of his steps remain to this day. The grizzlies went out to meet him by thousands; and, as he approached, they stood apart in two great lines, with their clubs under their arms, and so opened a lane by which he passed in great state to the lodge where his daughter sat with her children.

"But when he saw the children, and learned how the grizzlies that he had created betrayed him into the creation of a new race, he was very wroth, and frowned on the old mother grizzly till she died on the spot. At this, the grizzlies all set up a dreadful howl; but he took his daughter on his shoulder and, turning to all the grizzlies, bade them hold their tongues, get down on their hands and knees, and so remain until he returned. They did as they were bid, and he closed the door of the lodge after him, drove all the children out into the world, passed out and up the mountain, and never returned to the timber any more.

"So the grizzlies could not rise up any more, or use their clubs, but have ever since had to go on all-fours, much like the other beasts, except when they have to fight for their lives, when the Great Spirit permits them to stand up and fight with their fists like men.

"That is why the Indians about Mt. Shasta will never kill or interfere in any way with the grizzly. Whenever one of their number is killed by one of these kings of the forest, he is burned on the spot, and all who pass that way for years cast a stone on the place until a great pile is thrown up.

"In proof of the truth of the story that the grizzly once walked and stood erect, and much like man, they show that he has scarcely any tail, and that his arms are a great deal shorter than his legs, and that they are more like man than any other animal.

"This is the Indian legend of his creation, and since the legend must tell the truth, the whole truth and nothing but the truth, who can tell?"

Fig. 8- Famed Author Joaquin Miller
wrote about early legends of the Native Americans

THE MODOC INDIANS

MOUNT SHASTA, SISKIYOU COUNTY, CALIFORNIA—FROM A SKETCH BY OUR SPECIAL ARTIST

Fig. 9- Modoc Indians at Mount Shasta
When the wilds were really the wilds

Fig. 10- Aaron Stein (1853-1900), California and Oregon Stage Company.
Stagecoach Route in View of Mount Shasta

Fig. 11- Mount Shasta Over Pond, 1868 by John Henry Hill

History And Early Legends

The Los Angeles Times Prints The News

By Tim Cridland

Fig. 12- Tim Cridland

I had originally come across Tim Cridland, whose stage name is Zamora the Torture King, while prowling the world wide web. I am a member of a Yahoo group whose interests center on the Shaver Mystery and anything remotely involving the Inner and Hollow Earth Mysteries. I kept seeing the name "Zamora King" popping up and after a bit of investigation discovered who lurked behind this moniker.

When I sent out a notice on the Shaver list that I was planning to do a book on Mount Shasta and would welcome contributions, "The Torture King" offered his assistance.

Tim Cridland told me that he had found any number of references to this California landmark in none other than the "Los Angeles Times."

Interested readers can email Tim Cridland at ZamoraKing@aol.com. Also, Tim's book "Weird Las Vegas and Nevada" can be purchased directly from Tim by sending $20 postpaid to PO Box 71652, Las Vegas, NV 89170.

The concept of a sunken continent in the Pacific Ocean, called Lemuria or Mu, and that part of the West Coast of the United States, California in particular, is a remnant of this sunken land, was taken very seriously in the first part of the twentieth century. The existence of the sunken continent of the Pacific was discussed by scientists, spiritualists and laymen alike. In 1932, the Los Angeles Times published an oft quoted article, linking the lost land of Lemuria to Mount Shasta a look through the archives of the Los Angeles Times puts the article in context and shows how the public's perception of Lemuria and Mu has changed over the years.

The first two mentions of Lemuria in the Times were reprinted from other sources. The January 14, 1894 issue republished the article A Lost Continent from The Youths Companion. This short treatise mentions the lost continents of the Atlantic Ocean, Antipodea and Atlantis and then states "The other lost continent is an invention or deduction of modern science. It is called Lemuria...." The unattributed author writes that Lemuria is said to have been in the Indian Ocean, it further states that "According to some German savants, man himself probably originated in Lemuria instead of in Asia." This is tame stuff compared to the Times' next mention of Lemuria.

The Nov. 29, 1908 issue contained a lengthy article, Olden Times: Geographical Discoveries, which reads like a mash up of science, speculation and the theories of the Theosophists, who had taken the idea of Lemuria into their unorthodox history of mans evolution on earth. This article is also unattributed but it seems that most of its information came from "Mr. W. Scott Elliott, of London, who claims to had recourse to unusual sources of research..." It states that there have been three great cataclysmic events, caused by polar shifts, which have wiped out old continents and raised new ones, as well as the civilizations that inhabited them. It states that there have been five great continents in the history of Earth. "The Third Continent was Lemuria. The name was the invention of one P. L. Sclater, who between 1850 and 1860 asserted on zoological grounds the actual existence in prehistoric times of a continent which he showed to have extended from Madagascar to Ceylon and Sumatra. It included some portions of what is now Africa, but otherwise this gigantic continent, which stretched from the Indian Ocean to Australia, has now wholly disappeared below the waters of Pacific, leaving only here and there some its highland tops which are now islands." It quotes a scientist, "Prof. Schmidt," an advocate of Lemuria, who says that in addition the scientific findings, "...there is as evidence the most ancient traditions of various and widespread peoples, legends in India, in ancient Greece, Madagascar, Sumatra, Java and all the principle islands of Polynesia, as well as the legends of both Americas."

The article states that strange things in the human evolution occurred there. "It was in the Lemurian period that the separation of the sexes took place, the race until having being hermaphrodites..." Mentioning historic evidence of giant humans, including finding of apparent giant human fossilized footprints near Carson City, NV., the unknown author says "Man at that time was gigantic in bulk compared to with its present size." and more bizarrely: "Organs of vision were evolved in this third race, at first the single eye in the middle of the forehead, later called the third eye, and then the two eyes." The article is attributed to The Chicago Tribune. A check of the Tribune's files shows that they published this article in their July, 26, 1908 under the title How the World Looked Before the Flood and was part of a series of article that included one titled Lemuria: Mysterious Prehistoric Realm of the Scientists Disclosed by Hindu Sages.

Running parallel with the Lemurian origin of man, and the West coast of the US being the refuge of the first humans, was the theory that man began in the America, and that all the cultures and races spread out from America, not the other way round. Captain Alan LeBaron, who explored the Southwest from 1912 up to the 1930s, was a popular proponent of this theory in the 20s and 30s, although he is now almost completely forgotten.

A report published by the University of California Oakland summarized LeBaron's hypothesis: "Capt. Le Baron's investigations are based on the theory that the high plateau forming most of Nevada and parts of Utah and Arizona is the oldest land on earth. There are geological maps which show that this area has not been submerged under the sea for more than 40 million years. It is therefore argued that it the logical place to find the origin of man." In the nomenclature of paleo-geography, the study of ancient land masses, this area is known as Cascadia. LeBaron called the first humans "the Cascadian race." They migrated to other lands when the climate changed from a lush fertile land to its current arid condition, LeBaron theorized.

LeBaron wrote about his explorations and findings in the Jan 3, 1928 issue of the LA Times, and on this occasion, brought Lemuria into the picture: "Archeology, science of things old, points to the great Aztec calendar, stone and other Aztec works of art on the island of Rappa, a remnant of the lost continent of Lemuria, and calls attention to the fact that the first written language had its origin in the deserts of Western America."

The May 22, 1932 issue of the *LA Times* contained an article titled "A People of Mystery: Are They the Remnants of a Lost Race? Do They Posses a Fabulous Gold Treasure?" by Edward Lanser. Lanser describes taking a business trip by train from Los Angels to Portland. When the train passed Mount Shasta, while an insomniac Lanser was "Gazing upon its splendor," he "...suddenly perceived that the whole southern side of the mountain was ablaze with a strange, reddish-green light." Later asking the conductor if he knew the source of the light, he was told matter of factly that it was "'Lemurians, they hold ceremonies up there.'"

On his return trip, Lanser got off the train near Shasta to find out more about the lights and the Lemurians.

"I discovered the existence of a 'mystic village' on Mt. Shasta was an accepted fact." He wrote. Area residents "...all attested to the weird ritual that are performed on the mountain side at sunset, midnight and sunrise." During his stay, the light show continued: "...I have seen the midnight ceremonials cause the entire to be illuminated in the most baffling way-- a light that reaches up and covers the landscape for great distances."

Locals told him about sightings of the Lemurians. There were weird tales of there ability to camouflage themselves: "...if they desire, they can blend themselves into their surroundings and vanish." Their city is protected by an "invisible boundary" and told no one has ever been able to get into the city. Lanser repeats an unverified story that Edgar Larkin, a science writer who had previously written favorably about a Shasta/Lemurian connection, actually sighted the city on the side of the mountain with his high powered telescope.

Lanser repeats locals' descriptions of Lemurians as "...tall, barefoot, noble looking men, with close-cropped hair, dressed in spotless white robes that resemble in style the enveloping garment of the high-caste East Indian women today...," and most incredibly repeats claims that they sometimes buy goods from local merchants using gold nuggets for payment.

"The really incredible thing," wrote Lanser, "is that they have that these stanch decedents of that vanished race have succeeded in secluding themselves in the midst of our teeming State and that they have managed through some marvelous sorcery to keep highways, hot-dog establishments, filling stations and the other ugly counterparts of our tourist system out of their sacred precincts."

After this, the *LA Times* accounts of Lemuria when to back to a more scientific view. The May 20, 1934 edition carried the science column "What's New in the Progress of Science?" by Ransome Sutton. Under the heading

"Lemuria Located," Sutton discussed an expedition headed by Prof. Stanley Gardner, that succeeded in "mapping the mountains and valleys of Lemuria" under the Indian Ocean. "It is fortunate, the evolutionists believe, that Lemuria sank; otherwise primates might never have risen above the lemur level." Wrote Sutton, referring to the primates that gave Lemuria its name, "It was only a step from Lemuria to the Garden of Eden"

The Sep 4, 1934 issue got back to suggesting that Lemurian/Shasta connection in an article Our Expanding Universe by E. H. Whitehouse. The article presents the views of Wishare Cerve, the pen-name of Harve Spencer Lewis, who wrote the 1931 book Lemuria: The Lost Continent of the Pacific, which may have been a source for some of Lanser's article. The article got right to the point: "California... is a chip off the oldest block in creation--the lost continent of Lemuria!"

"Go east young Lemurian!" seemed to be the call, as Cerve is quoted saying that "'...the ancient people of Lemuria, finding their great continent submerging ... scattered into the valleys and mountainsides of this eastern portion of their continent which seemed to be rising higher.'" "Mr. Cerve contends that California, Washington, Oregon and Baja California, then formed an island separated from the North American Continent by a great inland sea, " wrote Whitehouse.

Lemuria had become interchangeable with Mu, the name that writer James Churchwood had given to a hypothetical sunken Pacific Continent, that he promoted in a widely read series of books. *LA Times* columnist Harry Carr wrote of Mu many times in the mid-1930s, sometime frivolously, sometimes seriously, but always with interest. The concept that humans originated from a sunken pacific continent had become so prevalent that the archaeologist Dr. Mark Harrington, of the Southwest Museum, who's own theories of humans cohabiting with prehistoric giant sloths were themselves unorthodox, felt compelled to quip, in an interview in the Aug. 7, 1932 issue, that "...we will wake up someday to find the law prohibiting us from teaching that man came from anywhere but from the island of Mu."

Mentions of Lemuria and Mu began to fade from the *LA Times* as the decades moved into the 40s and 50s. There were less articles and more announcements of lectures, some by scientists but most by the Rosicrucians and other spiritual organizations, and the majority of these being paid ads.

By the 1960s the concept of Lemuria had slipped beneath the mainstream, and belonged to occultist groups, and many of which were congregating at Mount Shasta.

Staff writer Charles Hillinger gave an overview of these groups, and the legends of drew them to Shasta in an article titled Mt. Shasta: The Lure of

Legend and Mystery in the 1, 1971 issue. In addition to reporting on the occultists near Shasta, and the how the locals react to them, he also informed his readers of another tribe that lives in Mount Shasta, distinct from the Lemurians, know as the Yaktayvians. "Legend has it that the Yaktayvians are the greatest bell makers on earth – that they hollowed out the mountain with the sounds of their bells and chimes," he wrote.

Hillinger would later report on a group called the Lemurian Fellowship, headquartered in Ramona, CA in the July 31, 1977 issue, in an article titled Mystery Cult Claims Wisdom of Mu. The Lemurian Fellowship had been around since 1936; its ads had appeared in the *LA Times* over the years, including some mentioning its knowledge of the Mount Shasta Lemurians. Their office, says Hillinger, has a map of the Lemuria/Mu that shows names and locations of geographical features, including the capital city "Hamukulia." The Lemurian Fellowship is still active at the time of this writing.

Lemuria got some bad press the Sept. 27, 1979 issue of the *LA Times*, when a bizarre sadistic killer claimed a connection. In the article Hulbert Shocks Court in Giving Message to Jury, reporter Jeffery Perlman writes that just before deliberations, when given a chance to say something to the jury, accused murderer and rapist Kenneth Hulbert uttered a bizarre phrase, "Iliasu Nogabugundu," which he claimed was 5000 years old. Later, when asked to explain what this meant, Hulbert stated in a written note that the phrase came originated with the "Lemurian Society," apparently something very different from the aforementioned Fellowship. He said the Lemurian Society originated around 3000 BC, but would not reveal what the phrase meant, although later he said it was a name of someone who he would not expose. After his conviction Hulbert stated that he feared he would be killed for saying the name in public.

From Hulbert's statements and actions, it would seem more likely that if he was in contact with an ancient, underground race it was probably Richard Shaver's Deros rather then the spiritually advance Lemurians.

Edward Lanser's Account in Retrospect

Since it publication in 1932, Edward Lanser's account of Lemurian activity on Mount Shasta has been reprinted and quoted numerous times; a source of validation for some and scorn to others. For all the discussion, few have attempted to find out who Edward Lanser was.

Edward Lanser's name appeared in the *LA Times* 12 times between 1924 and 1948. These mentions reveal that Lanser was a wealthily person, socially connected, with an active interest in the arts.

He was not a writer for The Times; the Mount Shasta article was his only feature. His name appears only twice before its publication. His first contribution to The Times was a flowery poem celebrating Hollywood, the next a letter poetically lamenting the passing of LA author Alice Harriman.

After the Shasta article, Lanser's name shows up in 2 society columns, as the author of 2 letters, in an article concerning the divorce trial of the daughter of a "department store magnate" and an Opera singer, in which he is described as a "family friend," and finally in a series of articles concerning his position in the California Art Club and his controversial views on abstract art.

Scoffers of Lanser's article have dealt with it in two ways; suggesting it is an outright falsehood or that Lanser is a pen-name for someone else, or acting on behalf of someone who has a socio/political stake in promoting the Shasta/Lemuria legends.

The first is the position taken by a writer for The New York Times, when reviewing the book The Problem of Lemuria by Lewis Spence in the April 2, 1933 edition. The reviewer chides Spence for "...not recognizing a bit of spoofing for what it evidently is..." when he reprinted a "...long quotation from a Pacific Coast paper of a year ago... ."

The second is the position taken by the author of a Mount Shasta Annotated Bibliography, viewable on the Internet.

The author notes great similarity Lanser's account and two earlier published accounts, one a Rosicrucian magazine article and another a chapter in a book. The bibliography's compiler suggests that they all "...were the work of one person or group of people."

The first assertion, that the article is spoof, has nothing to back it up, aside from The New York Times book reviewer's disbelief in the tale. the *LA Times* never retracted the story, they never said it was meant for entertainment, and Lanser's social standing never suffered for its telling; no one scolding him in a letter or in any other way, despite other controversies that he became involved in.

The second suggestion, that Lanser was a pen-name, does not stand up. His presence in the Times, before and after the article, show that he was a real person, and none indicate that he had any connection with Theosophists or Rosicrucians.

His political views, though strong, do not seem to have been unusual or extremist. But there is the troubling fact that some of what he wrote is very similar to the early articles, partially the descriptions of the Lemurians, Edgar Larkin's alleged sighting via telescope of the Lemurian city, and the habits of Lemurians purchasing goods with gold nuggets.

Rereading Lanser's account, there is a logical explanation for this. If you divide his account into what he experienced, and to what others told him, all of the descriptions of the Lemurians and their behavior were provided by other sources. Lanser says he saw the light display from the train, and when he returned to investigate, saw it on a nightly basis. This was his personal experience. He then went around the area asking about the lights, and the tales of the Lemurian colony. It would be surprising if someone did not suggest he read the already published accounts, which Lanser then incorporated into the tales the townspeople were telling him.

This in no way diminishes Lanser's experience. It would appear that Lanser, an educated, socially connected and respected member of his community, saw something very strange on his visit to the Mount Shasta vicinity. Lanser saw a regular light show that illuminated the side of the mountain with a "...display of light that far excels our modern electric achievements...." What he saw was so strange that the tales of the Lemurian colony were the only thing that could logically explain it.

Fig. 13- Arial photograph of Shasta on a gloomy day

Home of the Underground Dwellers and Ancient Gods

History And Early Legends

The White Man Comes To Mount Shasta

By James W. Moseley

Veteran researcher James Moseley has made a career out of being a modern-day Sherlock Holmes of Ufology and the paranormal. Starting his investigations in the 1950s, he still scans the sky for phantoms of the air and anything that happens to dwell between heaven and hell. For years, he ran an office on Fifth Avenue from which he published the "polished" (for its day) publication "Saucer News," with a readership approaching ten thousand. I was the managing editor for a period of a year or two.

James also held monthly meetings at various Times Square hotels and threw the largest indoor UFO convention of all time in 1967. Today, he makes his home in Key West, Florida, where he continues printing all the news that everyone else is afraid to touch in "Saucer Smear," a frequently issued newsletter aimed at the "inner circle" of saucerdom. He wrote this piece "awhile back" after being impressed with the stories he heard from his many subscribers.

*James is also the author of **Shockingly Close To The Truth,** which can be found on Amazon.com. Copies of "Saucer Smear" can be downloaded from www.UFOTV.com or by snail mail from James W. Moseley, Box 1709, Key West, FL 33041.*

Many books and stories have been written on the subject of Lost Civilizations - ancient races whose way of life was in many ways superior to ours today. But to me, the most fascinating of these tales concern ancient civilizations which are supposed to still be in existence.

Right here in the United States, the area surrounding Mount Shasta, California has been the cause of a great many legends. The "Mystery People" who are said to have lived there until very recently (and who may still be there), resent intrusion upon their privacy by outsiders, and there are many occasions when they have used their mystical powers to turn visitors away. There are several stories from the early days of the automobile, stating that when motorists would reach a certain point on the road, a light would flash before the startled eyes of the tourists, and the electrical system of their car would cease functioning. Not until the passengers emerged from the car and backed it down the road for a hundred feet or more would the engine regain its normal powers. The absence of such occurrences today would seem to indicate that the residents of the forests have died out at last, or have intermingled with the modern inhabitants of the region.

It is also claimed that on a number of occasions when great forest fires have raged in various parts of California and have approached close to the forest near Mount Shasta, a strange fog has suddenly emanated from the section occupied by these peculiar people; and this fog has risen from the ground in a circular manner so as to form a wall around the entire region, through which forest fires have never penetrated. Some natives in this area take delight in taking skeptics on a circular tour, pointing out to them the mute evidence shown by the burnt trees reaching a definite line that encloses the mysterious region. On the inside of this circle the trees rise to great heights, are of old age, and without a single scar or blemish from the burning of the trees that were destroyed within two hundred feet of them.

People living in that part of California also claim that strange cattle, unlike anything ever seen in America, have emerged from the woods, but before going very far along the highways and byways, these animals would be frightened by some invisible signal, and would abruptly turn around and run back toward the places from which they came.

Flying Saucers are a part of these legends too. However, the saucers are not disc shaped, but elongated like a cigar. In the old days, these "cigars" were called "aerial submarines" because of their resemblance in shape to a sub; but instead of going through the water, these mysterious vessels sailed through the air. However, they were equally capable of landing upon the ocean and acting like a conventional ship. This ability to fly through the air and land on water was not the only accomplishment of these vessels of the "Mystery People," for the "aerial submarines" could function like an ordinary submarine and travel under water, as well as dive to great depths under the ocean.

There are hundreds of people who have testified to having seen these peculiarly shaped boats flown out of the Mount Shasta region, high in the air over the hills and valleys of California. Similar boats have been seen by sailors on the high seas, and others have seen these "cigars" rise in the air and go upon the land of some of the islands of the Pacific. These peculiar vessels have been seen as far north as the Aleutian Islands.

In 1931 the following account was written: "Recently a group of persons playing golf on one of the golf links of California, near the foothills of the Sierra Nevada range, saw a peculiar silver-like vessel rise in the air, float over the mountaintops and disappear. It was unlike any airship that had ever been seen and there was absolutely no noise emanating from it to indicate that it moved by motor of any kind." The exact location of this golf link is not given, and thus the reference is vague, as is the case with so much of the material concerning Mount Shasta. However, if there is any truth to the saying "where there's smoke there's fire," then there must be some truth in these accounts concerning the "Mystery People."

The theory behind all this is that Mount Shasta is inhabited by a race of people who are survivors of the lost continent of Lemuria. Even in modern times, they have continued to manufacture their principal necessities, and have kept themselves carefully isolated from the outside world. One reason these people are not seen more often by outsiders is that they have constructed their city within the great mountain itself - or so the story goes. Only on rare occasions do they come outside, to hold their various tribal celebrations. There is said to be a tunnel through the eastern base of Mount Shasta, leading to a city of strange homes. The heat and smoke that can be seen arising from the crater of the mountain comes from the interior city. This is not an unusual tale, inasmuch as there are records showing that in Mexico other descendants of the Lemurians are living in an extinct volcano, hidden from all possible worldly observation.

(Editor's Notes In confirmation of the above, a story which appeared in the Feb. 10, 1980 issue of a San Francisco newspaper reported the story of a Mr. Jose Carmen Garcia, of Irapato, Mexico, who claimed that in 1947 he met a man who told him that he had been held captive in an underground city beneath a nearby volcano. This stranger was given a "magic formula" (a series of written symbols) by the underground inhabitants for growing giant vegetables. The stranger gave Garcia a copy of this formula and using the formula Garcia later went on to grow the largest vegetables ever recorded officially in that area. Also, there are reports of explorers who, while investigating the caves in Mt. Sombrero in the Tampico region of Mexico, claimed to have heard sounds emanating from deep within the cave which according to them sounded something similar to the sounds made by a "hydroelectric generating plant.")

Thus, if we are to believe the testimony of many reliable people, we are led to the possibility that a fascinating, totally unknown people lived in California until very recently. Whether these people continue to practice their ancient rites and live as they did, or whether they have finally adopted modern methods, is another unanswered question. It seems to me that some extremely valuable research could be done by anyone interested enough to visit the Mount Shasta area personally and investigate the truth of these stories.

Fig. 14- Artwork by Carol Ann Rodriguez
Miraculous healings are among the many unexplained occurrences
associated with Mount Shasta.

Fig. 15- Breathtaking Ariel View Taken June 2006 by Ewen Denney

Fig. 16- Diller Canyon on Mt Shastina Photo by Daniel Mayer October 2003

The Occult Connection

A DWELLER ON TWO PLANETS REMEMBERED

REVELATIONS OF GUY BALLARD AND THE "I AM" MOVEMENT

LITTLE LEMURIANS AND THE SHASTA RUBY

INSIDE THE HIDDEN DEPTHS OF MOUNT SHASTA

MOUNT SHASTA — I HAVE BEEN THERE!

Fig. 17 - "Siskiyou the Golden"
Yreka Newspaper, County Fair issue, circa 1920.

The Occult Connection

A Dweller On Two Planets Remembered

By Frederick Spencer Oliver

If anyone can take credit for being the first to pinpoint Mount Shasta as a metaphysical Mecca, that individual would have to be a youthful Frederick Spencer Oliver, who, while staking out the boundaries of his father's mining claim, started jotting down mesmerizing notes in a book he carried on his person. The notes were beautifully written, beyond poetic, and while reading them later, Oliver noted that they did not pertain to the mining claims he was supposed to be keeping a record of. Instead, the notes purported to be the musings of an invisible being who identified himself as a Lemurian scribe named Phylos.

*The being took over Oliver's hand on numerous occasions and assisted in penning a book that has become a metaphysical classic. **A Dweller On Two Planets** has been in print since 1895, and was actually one of the first books I can remember selling when I honed my profession as a bookseller at the age of seventeen. I sold dozens of copies and several publishers have made sure the book remains in print. The rather thick, sometimes ponderous work is rendered like a stream-of-consciousness dream. There are many prophetic references in **Dweller** and artwork not unlike what could be found in a modern day work of occultism. The drawings include depictions of cigar-shaped craft said to fly both in the air and under the waters. Most amazing is the fact that they look remarkably like the cigar-shaped ships photographed by contactee George Adamski through a telescope—many decades after the passing of Frederick Spencer Oliver.*

*Though there are numerous references to Mount Shasta in the pages of **Dweller On Two Planets**, perhaps the most appealing deal with the many stories told and retold concerning underground tunnels and chambers deep within the heart of Shasta. Those interested in the complete works of young Frederick should have no trouble finding the book to this day. We take a few appropriate excerpts that depict his arcane and esoterically written style to show how Mount Shasta has aided others in their search for knowledge and spiritual growth.*

Traveling, southward, miner no more, the youth bends his course. A year agone the golden phantoms died, the mine caved in, and "no man knows that sepulcher" in the wilds of Siskiyou. Winter wet had extinguished the flames, and laid the smoky sea. But the succeeding summer saw all aglow again, matched by the lightning of heaven. Our traveler is at the very base of Ieka Butte, and he and his steed crawl along the slopes and vales in the bed of the fire-born ocean of smoke as do crustaceans on the bottoms of aqueous seas. A flaw of wind decreases the denseness of the clouds, and above his head he sees an indistinct shape, lit feebly by the smoke-smothered moon, at its full now, as on that other night, a year ago. Beautiful through the murky air it is not; but when told that the point seen overhead is the smoke-free, gleaming crest of Shasta, fifteen miles away as the crow flies, e'en though we gaze at it from its own base, we feel an indescribable sense of awe. And we liken the mount, with the flaming forest glowing at its feet, and its own muffled form rising in obscured grandeur--to a silent sentinel by his watch fire, wrapped around with his cloak, and meditating on the trust he has kept--lo! these many ages, still keeps, and forever!

Returned from the far south, and in camp. In camp at the timber line on Tchastel's side, awaiting the nightfall, and through the long afternoon gazing out over a wealth of scenery not in word power to paint. To the north "Goose Nest" mountain--its crater ever full of fleecy snow--rears itself aloft eleven thousand feet. Down yonder in that gem-like valley is the lovely town of Sissons; down, to our traveler, albeit on a plane seven thousand feet above the ocean. Night. But not in a tent door. No, on mule-back, he and a companion are toiling upwards. There is no moon, no wind, no sound, save a few strange noises arising from the nether regions. No moon; yet plenty of light, since the snow seems self luminous, so that objects appear against it in sharp silhouette. How black the bleak rocks and ledges! And those glimmerings of light afar in the night--what are they? Lamps; lamps miles away, thousands of feet lower, yet in seeming not so far off. It is cold; oh, so frightfully cold, numbing the mind! And still--as the grave. No sounds now arise to the ear; 'tis too high for aught save silence. So cold; and yet mid-day sun heats reflect from the snows as from a mirror, and then the temperature is fearful to feel, yet the snow melts not. Here is a hot, sulphur spring, one thousand feet below the apex. Warm your chilled hands in the hot mud, wipe them quickly, lest they freeze, and climb on. Your eyes, could you see them, congested as they are in the rarified atmosphere, the color of liver, would horrify you. Your breathing pains you; your heart-beats sound like the thuds of a pile driver, your throat is afire from thirst. No matter; here is the top! Two o'clock a. m. in July, 188--. As yet no light, but faint dawn. But ere long the soul is awe-stricken by a weird glow in the east, which lights nothing. The beholders are filled with a strange disquiet; see the waxing light, and--in fear and wonder, almost terror--see the great sun, scarce heralded by the aerial rarity, spring from beneath the horizon. Yet all below is in "the darkest hour before the dawn." No ridges, no hills appear, no valleys, nothing but "night's deep darkness." We seem to have lost the world, and, for the nonce, are free of time! The planet is swallowed up, leaving the mountain top's half acre sole visible spot of all the Universe, save only the fearful splendor of Helios. Understand now, for you may, the sensations of Campbell's "last man." The world all gone, and self and comrade alone on a small spot in mid-air, whereon the almost rayless sun casts cold beams of strange, weird brightness. Look north. Afar in the night are four cones of light--Mt. Hood, Mt. Adams, Mt. Tacoma, and St. Helen's tall torch, all peers of our Ieka. As the Day King soars higher lesser peaks appear, then long black ridges--ranges of vast extent--begin near by, only to lose themselves in distant darkness.

Now the void of night vanishes, hills stand forth, silvery spots and streaks appear as the dawn lights lakes and rivers, and at last, no fog obscuring, in the distant west, seventy miles away, is seen the great gray plain, the Pacific's broad expanse. To the south interrupted streaks of silver show where flow Pitt and Sacramento rivers, while over two hundred miles away behold an indentation of California's central coast, marking the Golden Gate, and San Francisco's world-famed bay.

Beside a roaring, dashing mountain torrent--falling in myriad cascades of foam white as drifted snow, interspersed with pools of quiet water--deep, trout-filled, blue, reflecting flowery banks and towering pine-crested ridges, "ribbs of the planet," we pause. The day is hot, but the waters of this branch of McCloud river are cold as the pristine snows of Shasta from which they flow to our feet and thence away.

We recline on the brink of a deep blue crystal pool, idly casting pebbles into the shivering image of a tall basalt cliff reflected from the mirror-calm surface.

What secrets perchance are about us! We do not know as *we* lie there, our bodies resting, our souls filled with peace, nor do we know until many years are passed out through the back door of time that that tall basalt cliff conceals a doorway. We do not suspect this, nor that a long tunnel stretches away, far into the interior of majestic Shasta. Wholly unthought is it that there lie at the tunnel's far end vast apartments--the home of a mystic brotherhood, whose occult arts hollowed that tunnel and mysterious dwellings--"Sack" the name is. Are you incredulous as to these things? Go there, or suffer yourself to be taken as I was, once! See, as I saw, not with the vision of flesh, the walls, polished as by jewelers, though excavated as by giants; floors carpeted with long, fleecy gray fabric that looked like fur, but was a mineral product; ledges intersected by the builders, and in their wonderful polish exhibiting veins of gold, of silver, of green copper ores, made afar from the maddening crowd, a refuge whereof those who, "Seeing, see not," can truly say:

"And no man knows..."
"And no man saw it e'er."

Once I was there, friend, casting pebbles in the stream's deep pools; yet it was then hid, for only a few are privileged. And departing, the spot was forgotten, and today, unable as any one who reads this, I cannot tell the place. Curiosity will never unlock that secret. Does it truly exist? Seek and ye shall find; knock and it shall be opened unto you. Shasta is *a* true guardian and silently towers, giving no sign of that within her breast. But there is a key. The one who first conquers self, Shasta will not deny.

This is the last scene. You have viewed the proud peak both near and far; by day, by night; in the smoke and in the clear mountain air; seen its interior and from its apex gazed upon it and the globe stretched away beneath your feet. 'Tis a sight of God's handwork, sublime, awful, never-to-be-forgotten; and as thy soul hath sated itself with admiration thereof, in that measure be now filled with His Peace.

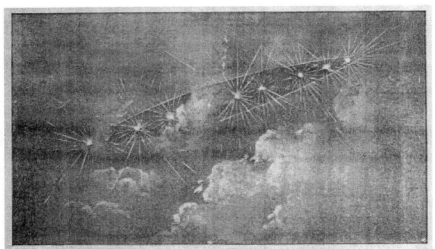

Fig. 18 - One of the drawings in A Dweller On Two Planets
resembles the famous mother ship UFOs photographed by the late contactee

Fig. 19 - 2ND of the drawings in A Dweller On Two Planets
similar to the large mother ships seen and photographed

The Occult Connection

Revelations of Guy Ballard and the "I Am" Movement

By Arthur Francis Eichorn, Sr.

*Arthur Francis Eichorn Sr. passed away in 1954. He is best known for his series of articles that were collected and included in the book **The Mount Shasta Story: Being a Concise History of the Famous California Mountain.***

The "I AM" chapter of the Mt. Shasta Story was in many ways a most difficult one to compile. During my initial research into this unusual story, I was confronted with many distorted fragments of hearsay that very nearly discouraged my attempt to include this important and certainly integral portion of the mountain's past. The local citizens of the Mt. Shasta region had many varied versions of what was known as the "Saint Germain Legend," yet few, if any, were near the truth. The story in its original form was truly amazing but the invented variations were pure conjecture, elaborated beyond recognition with each telling.

Local interest in the "I AM" group began in the year 1934 with the publication of a book entitled "Unveiled Mysteries" written by Godfre Ray King. The author was actually the late Mr. Guy W. Ballard, founder of the world famous Saint Germaine Foundation. The origin of the nom de plume "Godfre Ray King" was derived according to Mrs. G. W. Ballard as follows: "The God Free Ray is King, which means, the flame of God's own heart, which we know as the Great Central Sun, which is the Great Sun behind our Physical Sun."

In his book, Mr. Ballard revealed a truly astounding experience that not only affected local citizens of the Mt. Shasta region, but also deeply affected the vast membership of the "I AM" Activity. The members of this group, who at one time numbered over twelve million, are widely scattered. The membership consists of people from every state in the Union as well as people in Europe and large numbers in New Zealand, Australia, Switzerland, Scotland and South Africa.

Fig. 20 - Guy Ballard
is believed to have been among the first to speak of
Lemurians residing on Mount Shasta

Since the original story of Mr. Ballard's experience on Mt. Shasta during the summer of 1930 has become distorted and disparaged by local waggery, I will attempt to correct these deceptions for the layman by briefly quoting directly from the original form with the gracious permission of Mrs. G.W. Ballard. So without further comment, I offer the original version of Mr. Ballard's strange and unusual experience.

"Unveiled Mysteries" was written according to Mr. Ballard, "...in the embrace of the majestic, towering presence of Mt. Shasta, whose apex is robed forever in that pure, glistening White, the symbol of the 'Light of Eternity.'

"I had been sent on Government business to a little town situated at the foot of the mountain, and while thus engaged, occupied my leisure time trying to unravel this rumor concerning The Brotherhood. I knew, through travels in the Far East, that most rumors, myths, and legends have, somewhere as their origin, a deep underlying Truth that usually remains unrecognized by all but those who are "real" students of life.

"I fell in love with Shasta and each morning, almost involuntarily, saluted the Spirit of the Mountain and the members of the Order. I sensed something very unusual about the entire locality and, in the light of the experiences that followed, I do not wonder that some of them cast their shadows before.

"Long hikes on the trail had become my habit, whenever I wanted to think things out alone or make decisions of serious import. Here, on this great Giant of Nature, I found recreation, inspiration, and peace that soothed my soul and invigorated mind and body.

"I had planned such a hike, for pleasure as I thought, to spend some time deep in the heart of the mountain, when the following experience entered my life, to change it so completely that I could almost believe I were on another planet, but for my return to the usual routine in which I had been engaged for months.

"The morning in question, I started out at daybreak deciding to follow where fancy led, and in a vague sort of way, asked God to direct my path. By noon, I had climbed high up on the side of the mountain where the view to the south was beautiful as a dream.

"As the day advanced, it grew very warm and I stopped frequently to rest and enjoy to the full the remarkable stretch of country around the McCloud River, Valley, and town. It came time for lunch, and I sought a mountain spring for clear, cold water. Cup in hand, I bent down to fill it, when an electrical current passed through my body from head to foot.

"I looked around, and directly behind me stood a young man who, at first glance, seemed to be someone on a hike like myself. I looked more closely, and realized immediately that he was no ordinary person. As this thought passed through my mind, he smiled and addressed me saying.

"'My Brother, if you will hand me your cup, I will give you a much more refreshing drink than spring water.' I obeyed, and instantly the cup was filled with a creamy liquid. Handing it back to me, he said, 'Drink it.' I did so, and must have looked my astonishment. While the taste was delicious, the electrical vivifying effect in my mind and body made me gasp with surprise. I did not see him put anything into the cup, and I wondered what was happening.

"'That which you drank,' he explained, 'comes directly from the Universal Supply, pure and vivifying as life itself, in fact it is Life - Omnipresent Life -for it exists everywhere about us. It is subject to our conscious control and direction, willingly obedient, when we Love enough, because all of the Universe obeys the behest of Love. Whatsoever I desire manifests itself, when I command in Love. I held out the cup, and that which I desired for you appeared. See! I have but to hold out my hand and, if I wish to use gold - gold is here.' Instantly, there lay in his palm a disc about the size of a ten dollar gold piece. Again he continued:

"'I see within you a certain Inner understanding of the Great Law, but you are not outwardly aware of it enough to produce that which you desire direct from the Omnipresent Universal Supply. You have desired to see something of this kind so intensely, so honestly, and so determinedly, it could no longer be withheld from you.

"'However, precipitation is one of the least important activities of the Great Truth of Being. If your desire had not been free from selfishness and the fascination of phenomena, such an experience could not have come to you. When leaving home this morning, you thought you were coming on a hike, that is, so far as the outer activity of your mind was concerned. In the deeper, larger sense you were really following the urge of your Inner God Self that led to the person, place, and condition wherein your most intense desire could be fulfilled.

"'The Truth of Life is, you cannot desire that which is not possible of manifestation somewhere in the Universe. The more intense the "feeling" within the desire, the more quickly it will be attained. However, if one be foolish enough to desire something that will injure another of God's children, or any other part of His Creation, then that person will pay the penalty in discord and failure, somewhere in his own Life's experience.' "

In Mr. Ballard's book, "Unveiled Mysteries," the learned stranger continues for many pages to reveal the great eternal law of life to Mr. Ballard. And then he commanded:

"Sit still for a few moments - watch me closely - and I will reveal my identity to you."

Mr. Ballard relates "I did as he requested and in perhaps a full minute, I saw his face, body, and clothing become the living, breathing, tangible 'Presence' of the Master, Saint Germaine, smiling at my astonishment and enjoying my surprise.

"He stood there before me - A Magnificent God-like figure - in a white jeweled robe, a Light and Love sparkling in his eyes that revealed and proved the Dominion and Majesty that are his." This, in the words of Mr. Ballard, was the first of many meetings with Saint Germain. The second meeting took place a few days later. Mr. Ballard arrived at the trysting place first and sat on a log waiting the arrival of Saint Germain.

"As I contemplated the wonderful privilege and blessing that had come to me, I heard a twig crack and looked around expecting to see him. Imagine my surprise, when not fifty feet away, I saw a panther - slowly approaching. My hair must have stood on end. I wanted to run, to scream - anything - so frantic was the feeling of fear within me. It would have been useless to move, for one spring from the panther would have been fatal to me.

Fig. 21 - Artist Carol Ann Rodriguez depicts life on Lemuria as she envisions it

"My brain whirled so great was my fear, but one idea came through clearly and held my attention steady. I realized that I had the Mighty 'Presence of God' right within me, and that this 'Presence' was all Love. This beautiful animal was part of God's Life also, and I made myself look at it, directly in the eyes. Then came the thought that one part of God could not harm another part. I was conscious of this fact only.

"A feeling of love swept over me, and went out like a Ray of light directly to the panther and with it went my fear. The stealthy tread ceased and I moved slowly toward it, feeling that God's Love filled us both. The Vicious glare in the eyes softened, the animal straightened up, and came slowly to me, rubbing its shoulder against my leg. I reached down and stroked the soft head. It looked up into my eyes for a moment and then, lay down and rolled over like a playful kitten. The fur was a beautiful dark, reddish brown: the body long, supple and of great strength. I continued to play with it and when I suddenly looked up, Saint Germaine stood beside me.

"'My Son,' he said, 'I saw the great strength within you or I would not have permitted so great a test. You have conquered fear. My congratulations! Had you not conquered the outer-self, I would not have allowed the panther to harm you, but our association would have ceased for a time.

"'I did not have anything to do with the panther being there. It was part of the Inner operation of the Great Law, as you will see before the association with your new-found friend ceases. Now, that you have passed the test of courage, it is possible for me to give much greater assistance. Each day you will become stronger, happier, and express much greater freedom.

"He held out his hand, and in a moment there appeared four little cakes of a beautiful golden brown, each about two inches square. He offered these and I ate them at his direction. They were most delicious. Immediately, I felt a quickening, tingling sensation through my entire body - a new sense of health and clearness of mind. Saint Germain seated himself beside me and my instructions began."

The teaching and instructions thus obtained from Saint Germain became the decrees and doctrines which were in turn later passed on to the membership of the "I AM" Activity of the Saint Germaine Foundation, by the special appointed messenger, Mr. Ballard.

In the preface of "Unveiled Mysteries," plans were quietly inaugurated to establish a permanent headquarters for the "I AM" Youth Foundation in the town of Mount Shasta. Special envoys were sent into the region to purchase property. In the first year $60,000 was spent in this way.

While searching through the archives in the files of local newspaper offices, I noted that this new influx of spending did not in all cases inspire welcome. In some quarters it induced a feeling of envy, suspicion, and resentment. Thus was born a campaign of persecution against the "I AM" membership. Unfounded rumors were manufactured, accusing these people of many weird and fantastic acts. It was felt by these gossiping groups, that people who did not eat meat, or flesh in any form, did not smoke or drink intoxicants, dressed in clothing of pastel colors, minded their business, bothered no one, were people to conjure about. This slanderous campaign continued for several years. In 1948, Mrs. G. W. Ballard was the special guest of the Mount Shasta Chamber of Commerce. She was invited to this meeting to explain the functions of the "I AM" Activity. Over two hundred citizens attended to hear this interesting talk. Again and again Mrs. Ballard emphasized that the work of her group was constructive and that their aim was to better the world through construction and beauty. She gave a slight insight into their beliefs and doctrines. She said that theirs were based upon the "universal energy and the power from above, also these beliefs are based on the Christian Bible."

Speaking of persecution, she said, "that many have been persecuted, including Jesus," but that "He came out all right." In referring to the prevalent rumors around Mount Shasta, she declared, "...that people talk most about what they know least."

At one time in the questioning the inquiries became very pointed, and President Jack Hammond reminded the audience that the meeting was for the purpose of learning of the business relations only, and was not a religious discussion.

Time wore on in the Mount Shasta region, and a trend toward acceptance developed. This feeling expanded to a full manifestation of acceptance in the late summer of 1955. This was the year that the general public was invited by Mrs. Ballard to attend the pageant presented by the students of the "I AM" Activity each year at the conclusion of their annual Conclave. The setting in 1955 was the beautiful amphitheatre located on upper McCloud Avenue, just outside the town of Mount Shasta. A crown of over 1,000 witnessed the thrilling and beautifully presented pageant depicting the Life of Christ. To say that the crowd was awed would be mild praise. Many were actually stunned at the beauty and the perfection of the presentation. The final scene was of Jesus' ascension. He climbed a winding path up the hillside back of the stage, said a few final words to the assembled angels and multitude below. Then on an ingeniously concealed elevator that appeared as a stately pine, he rose skyward and disappeared in a flash of light.

This was followed by a final address by Mrs. Ballard after which she and her official family carried the American flag to the ascension lift and had it born aloft as a symbol of America's ascension as a nation.

On September 1, 1955, seventeen business concerns of Mount Shasta purchased a full page advertisement in the Herald, thanking the "I AM" Activity for the invitation, and warmly praising the group on the majestic portrayal presented.

This pageant is presented each summer during the month of August in the beautiful amphitheatre on Quail Hill, and people travel thousands of miles to witness this never-to-be-forgotten portrayal of the Life of Christ.

Thus we have, in brief form, the "I AM" Story. True, it is not the complete story; it would take several volumes to present all the facts, but I anticipate that in my small way I have helped to present the true facts, explaining why the people of the "I AM" Activity look upon Mt. Shasta with special symbolic significance. For here it was that their founder met the ascended master - Saint Germain.

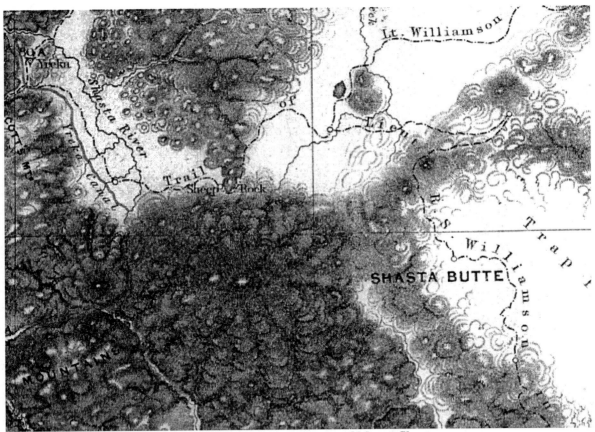

Fig. 22 - Topographical Layout of Mount Shasta

The Occult Connection

Little Lemurians and the Shasta Ruby

By Garth Sanders and Paul Doerr

If you see a little man with an extra eye in the middle of his forehead, call Harold Campbell, manager of the United California Bank here (ie. in Weed, California -Ed.).

The little man is probably a Lemurian and Campbell is investigating Lemurians. And some experts say Lemurians have three eyes (Editors notes Actually this "third" eye was not an "eye" in the literal sense, but in fact an extrasensory organ, as was mentioned earlier in this work - Ed.).

Ever since a woman told a nation-wide television audience about the Lemurians on the Art Linkletter show weeks ago (this article appeared in May 4, 1964 - Ed.), letters have streamed into the Weed Chamber of Commerce asking about the Lemurian legend.

The chamber delegated Campbell to look into the Lemurians.

"I'm thinking!" Campbell said mysteriously when I (Garth Sanders) asked him Thursday about his project.

He explained that the Lemurian legend "is all tied up in the story"

I read this story of Mu two years ago and I also studied geology and I suggest you do of Mu the same.

"You've seen pictures of Easter Island?" he asked, more mysterious than ever. "You read the story of Mu and you get a fairly good explanation of what could have happened. There is a theory that at one time there was an almost connected land mass all the way from Asia to North and South America.

"...Sometime during an exceptionally heavy earth movement this land mass dropped completely out of sight," Campbell postulated.

This was the continent of Mu, as any student of pseudo history knows. It is supposed to have been inhabited by a highly civilized race. When the continent was permanently dunked in the Pacific Ocean, most of the Lemurians drowned.

But a few escaped and settled deep in the bowels of Mt. Shasta.

Campbell saw the Linkletter television show himself. He says (with an air of intrigue) that Linkletter got a peculiar look on his face when the woman he was interviewing said she had seen Lemurians and offered to describe one for the audience.

Linkletter terminated the interview before the woman could describe a Lemurian, Campbell says.

What is Campbell doing toward getting in touch with Lemurians himself?

"I've been thinking," is all he will say about that.

Somehow after listening to Campbell you get the idea that the Lemurians may turn out to be the best friends the Weed Chamber of Commerce ever had.

Not everyone in Weed shares Campbell's open-minded attitude.

Fred Stratton, who has lived in Weed since 1915, says of the Lemurian legend, "It's mythological, like Zeus."

Stratton says he lived in a cabin high on Mt. Shasta for two years and guided tourists to the top of the mountain five times during 1915.

He emphatically says he never saw hide nor hair of a Lemurian, although he had heard rumors of them.

The Lemurian legend really picked up steam during prohibition when Weed bootleggers manufactured a moonshine whisky still remembered for its hallucinatory qualities, Stratton thinks.

"You can see purple hens after drinking that stuff," Stratton says.

Still the letters from the curious continue to puzzle the Chambers of Commerce of

Still, the letters from the curious continue to puzzle the Chambers of Commerce of Weed and Mount Shasta City. A letter from a St. Petersburg, Florida, woman says, "I listened to an interview on TV of a lady who was going to Mount Shasta, under which she claimed is an eight-miles-deep city of living people . . . I have told this to people who are skeptical."

A Tampa, Fla., woman wrote the Mount Shasta Chamber:

"I am especially interested in the making contact with the Theo-Christie Adepts of the Order of Azariah whose address has been given me as Shasta City, Calif."

Harold Campbell has plenty to keep him thinking . . .

Another interesting account from Mt. Shasta was related by Paul Doerr, editor of PIONEER (225 E. Utah, Fairfield, CA 94533 . Doerr's discovery of a strange "Ruby" on the slopes of Shasta is described by him as follows:

Several years ago while exploring the lower-middle slopes on the northern face of Mount Shasta (perhaps WWN - above a field of odd, breast-high, succulents or what looked like succulents, yet they obviously survive the winters) I found a large faceted sphere about 2 inches in diameter. Many tiny facets covered the surface of the crystal-like material of ruby color. It appeared fractured in places, and unfortunately I showed the "ruby" to a person who examined it, squeezed it, and it shattered into tiny fragments and several larger pieces. Some of the remains are now in Lawrence's Mystery Village Museum (Indiana?), along with some other stuff I picked up (some coins from Delphi), etc.

"Near the place where I discovered the artifact, there are some small cave-mouths, mostly hidden or buried - I followed a ground squirrel to one of them. Incidentally, that is the best way to find a hidden/buried/collapsed cave-mouth, follow a snake, burrow-bird, mouse, or some burrow-animal. Carry some wire or a stick and poke around. If there seems to be more hole than the particular animal would need, make like a groundhog and dig...'"

Fig. 23 - Early Days Near the Mountain

Fig. 24 - Leslie's Illustrated Newspaper

Fig. 25 - Mount Shasta Lake

The Occult Connection

Inside The Hidden Depths of Mount Shasta

By Bruce Walton

*No other author has compiled and written more than Bruce Walton when it comes to the mysteries surrounding the Inner and Hollow Earth, as well as subterranean cities and their vast tunnel system said to exist throughout the center of the Earth. All interested readers who want an endless amount of material on these subjects need only go to the Google search engine and type in the name "Branton" (Walton's alter ego). Hundreds of pages will immediately pop up linking to an assortment of "subterranean" sites where Walton attracts a daily readership in the thousands. Some of Bruce Walton's physical books are titled **Omega Files** and **The Majolica Desert Experience**.*

Hidden beneath the ancient, restless seas there lie the mysteries of forgotten civilizations. Worn away by terrific pressure, swept by the tides and half buried in the sands are the remnants of a culture little known today. Where the mighty Pacific ocean now rolls in its majestic sweep of thousands of miles, there is said to have at one time existed a vast continent known as Lemuria.

Modern day man prides himself on his so-called high level of civilization, unknowing that long before him other races of man grew and prospered, attained heights of scientific achievement and knowledge which would put our modern day scientists to shame, and finally disappeared so completely that all which remained were the strange myths and unexplained enigmas such as the Bimini road and the mysterious, majestic statues of Easter Island, as well as other ancient sites which have recently come to light.

Here on the great continent of Lemuria, existed one of the world's oldest civilizations, the people of which were possessed of supernatural powers and learning. During the cataclysmic geological changes in the surface of the earth, this great continent slowly began to sink into the waters of the Pacific. At this time, those who were aware enough to see the handwriting on the wall, so to speak, set out in a great migration in order to save themselves from the cataclysms which they knew were imminent. Many of the wise ones of Lemuria built time capsules in which they placed the benefit of their knowledge and many of their great inventions so that all may not be lost, but that a record of their existence might survive. They believed that one day, when the time was right, mankind would again discover this knowledge and use it for the benefit of all man, as well as have a complete record of those who had come before them. According to the legend, several areas of the world were chosen as sites for these great time capsules. Some of these sites included Central America, the Andes Mountains, Egypt, and even North America. In fact, one of the largest of these time capsules was built in the interior of what is now known as Mt. Shasta, in northern California. According to the legend, Mt. Shasta was once a part of the ancient continent of Lemuria, as was most of the state of California and parts of Nevada and Utah. At that time, the eastern flank of the great continent existed where the present day cascade range lies, being separated from the main body of North America by an inland sea, or Bonneville Sea which filled that area between the Sierra Nevada's and the western base of the Rocky Mountains several thousands of years ago.

Seeing that Mt. Shasta and the surrounding regions survived the deluge, many of the surviving Lemurians took refuge within the hollow interior of the mountain itself, and built there a city using their great skills and knowledge of engineering. Here, it is said, they live to this day, a rather reticent people who now wish only to live their independent existence until such a time when they feel that mankind has evolved to a level of responsibility which would make it possible for the Lemurians to make themselves widely known, and able to share their knowledge with the outer world without the fear that it might be used against them, or that man in his arrogance might use this knowledge self-destructively.

Mt. Shasta is located at the northern extremity of the Sierra Nevada range, and is the cone of an extinct volcano (although some geologists would probably label it "dormant") and rises to a height of over 14,380 feet above sea level. Scientists believe that it was at one time much higher than at present, and possibly even the highest peak in California, at one time. To the east of this volcano is the well-known Shasta Forest, the heart of which lies less than thirty miles from the base of the mountain. It is from this region which lies between the Forest and the base of the mountain that many strange tales have emerged. Among these are the reports are strange-looking people who would be seen to emerge from the forests and dense growths of trees in that region, only to run back into hiding after realizing that they were being observed. These same individuals, who were often described as tall, graceful, and agile, having the appearance of being quite old and yet exceedingly virile, were often seen in the early days entering the small towns surrounding the mountain, where they would trade gold nuggets or gold dust for some modern commodities, and in almost every case, these oddly dressed people would pay much more for the items than they were actually worth, as if the gold they possessed held no real value to them.

At other times, reports of unusual fires which gave off a blue and white illumination deep in the center of the forests would surface. Between the fire and the observer strange figures could be seen to pass at times. And, if the wind were blowing in the proper direction, strange chanting and singing, accompanied by weird, beautiful music would float or be carried in the direction of one of the small nearby towns.

Any attempt by an investigator to progress toward the strange lights and sounds would end in the observer coming in contact with a large heavily clad and concealed person who would simply lift up the curious party and turn him in the opposite direction, or at other times the observer would encounter an invisible force which would prevent any further progress. Both of these experiences have been reported by those who have witnessed these strange ceremonies. Others reported that as they neared the light they would suddenly find that they would get the sudden desire or urge to leave the place as fast of possible, an urge so strong that they could not resist it.

The Strange People of the Mountain

Several years ago there appeared a report of a very old man who emerged from this same area and proceeded to make some sort of important journey on foot to the City of San Francisco, where he was met by a committee of wealthy men at the Ferry Building and escorted up Market Street to the City Hall. Here some special ceremony was held to which all strangers were forbidden. Many of those who observed character being escorted said that never in all their lives had they seen a being of such nobility, humility, and majestic bearing in one expression. Who this strange man was or what he came to do was never revealed and even the date of the incident was denied to all investigators. Many such representatives of this hidden community at the foot of Mt. Shasta, or within it, have been seen on the highways unexpectedly, garbed in pure white and in sandals, with long curly hair, tall and majestic in appearance, but wholly undesirous of public attention.

During the "midnight" ceremonies of these strange people, witnesses claim to have seen several hundreds of individuals around these fires, and at times strange beams of lights are seen shining into the sky, sometimes catching a low hanging cloud, or illuminating strange dome-shaped buildings of marble and onyx. A strange stone monolith which had been discovered on the outskirts of the forest was engravers with strange hieroglyphic-type writings as well as an English translation which reads "CEREMONY OF ADORATION TO GUATAMA". It was also apparent from the writings that the ceremonies occurred at sunrise, sunset, and midnight and that the word "Guatama" referred to the continent of North America.

As an interesting note, experts who have studied the archaeological evidence in the Mt. Shasta district have proven that among many of the symbols to be found on stones and carved on walls made of stone or on the mountainsides themselves, there is an ancient mystical emblem of the Druidic lamp--used only by the ancient Druids and found nowhere else among the sacred and mystical symbolism.

The Astronomer's Tale

As possible confirmation of this hidden city at the base of Mt. Shasta was given by the famous astronomer Dr. Edgar Lucian Larkin, a former director of the Mt. Lowe observatory, who later went on to write extensively on Mt. Shasta after his experience, including a series of articles in the San Francisco EXAMINER.

One day, he wrote, while experimenting with a new telescope on an unnamed mountain peak in Northern California, he set about testing its daytime usefulness as well as to gauge a new standard scale for determining distances. He was aware at the time of the Mt. Shasta - Lemurian legend, but had never heard a satisfactory explanation to the mystery.

On one particular evening, he chose Mt. Shasta as an object upon which to focus his telescope, as the high snow-capped top of Shasta stood out clearly against the deep blue sky. After consulting a map of California in order to determine the exact distance between himself and the peak of Shasta, he made some notations for the purpose of comparing these figures with the new scale of relative distances upon which he was working. He later adjusted his telescope so that it included lower parts of Mt. Shasta and, expecting to see only the treetops which were spread out in the foreground between him and Shasta, he was startled to see an unusual glimmering curved surface. As the sun shone upon this glittering object which could make out among the trees he was impressed with the thought that he was looking at a gold-tinted dome of some type of Oriental building. He made observations and notations every twenty minutes or so, and as the sun moved in its course across the sky its rays revealed that there were two domes rising above the treetops in the vicinity of Mt. Shasta, and that several hundred feet distant from those, parts of a third dome could be made out. Making another minor adjustment of his telescope his eye caught the corner of another structure which was seemingly made of marble. Fully realizing that there were no such structures to his knowledge in Northern California, and especially in the forested regions surrounding the base of Mt. Shasta, he left his telescope fixed in its position in order to determine whether or not these strange structures were visible after sunset. He was surprised to find later in the night that around the domes were great lights, apparently white, which partially illuminated them, making them visible even though there was no moon to cast any light at the time.

Making precise notations of each peculiar thing which impressed him he waited for sunrise to make further observations. Looking closer, he was able to see smoke rising up between the trees as well as a portion of yet another structure. After one week's study of the matter he decided to investigate further, and it was his personal investigations which led many persons to explore the region around this mysterious mountain.

Early Histories of Mount Shasta

Mt. Shasta was also the home of several Indian tribes, these included the Okwanutou and Wintun's who lived on the south of the mountain; the Acho-Mawi who resided mainly on the south-east; the Modoc who dwelt on the north-east, and the Shasta Indians who inhabited the northern and western flanks.

The origin of the name "Shasta" is not entirely certain. One source claims that the Shasta Indians were named after the mountain, and not the other way around as one might expect, and that the name is of Russian derivation. It is claimed that the Russians who settled at Bodega on the coast, could see Mt. Shasta from the summit of the coast range and thereby named it "Tchastal;" or the white or pure mountain. This name the early Americans are supposed to have adopted, spelling, and pronouncing it Chaster, later substituting the soft SH for the hard CH.

According to another source, the Spaniards were the first to discover the mountain (first Europeans, that is), which they named "Jesus-Maria". The name Jesus probably denoted Shasta itself while the name Maria probably indicated the smaller twin peak, known today as Shastina.

However, according to the early historian Stephen Powers, the mountain was actually named after the Shas-ti-ka Indians, the tribal name for a group of Indians who lived in the Mt. Shasta region. The Shas-ti-ka Indians had their own name for the snowy mountains, and Shasta in particular, which was Wai-ri-ka, or, more correctly, Wai-i-ka.

One of the first accounts written by white man, concerning the mysterious people inside the mountain, was an occult novel titled A DWELLER ON TWO PLANETS, written by a Yreka, California youth named Frederick Spencer Oliver. The bulk of the book, as well as his later book AN EARTH DWELLER RETURNS, was reportedly dictated to Oliver via automatic writing by "Phylos the Thibetan". Phylos, who claimed to have lived during previous incarnations on Atlantis and Venus, also told Oliver of an incarnation which he had during the California gold rush. It was during this later incarnation as a man by the name of Walter Pierson, that Phylos encountered a mystic adept who passed as a Chinese laborer, and whose name was Quong. Quong led Walter Pierson into Mt. Shasta via a concealed tunnel and showed him the magnificent chambers and wonderful treasures of a mystical brotherhood who dwelt there in the mountain's interior for many ages, wielding awesome powers and sharing strange secrets while working always in obscure ways for the spiritual betterment of mankind. Although A DWELLER ON TWO PLANETS was written between 1883 and 1886, it did not see print until 1899.

The next major revelation on Mt. Shasta came in the form of a book titled LEMURIA: LOST CONTINENT OF THE PACIFIC, written by Harvey Spencer Lewis under the pen name of Wishar S. Cerve in the year 1931, and published by the Rosicrucian order (AMORC) of San Jose, California. Cerve's book, according to his statements in the introduction, was based largely upon ancient manuscripts which were brought to the United States from the ancient archives of China and Tibet. According to Lewis, long ago when the mighty continent of Lemuria was submerged in a cataclysm, its eastern edge pushed up against the western shore of North America to form most of what are now the states of Washington, Oregon and California. Among the many surviving remnants of this lost continent were those who sought refuge within the hollow interior of Mt. Shasta.

About this same time, a Dr. M. Doreal, the late coordinator of the Brotherhood of the White Temple, of Sedalia, Colorado, gave a series of lectures in Los Angeles on Mt. Shasta, which were later the basis for a pamphlet which he later wrote titled "Mysteries of Mt. Shasta". In this pamphlet, Doreal claims to have visited the dwellers at their colony inside the mountain. Two of these, he maintained, had attended his Los Angeles lectures back in the early 1930's. These two then took Doreal into their city by occult means, a city located about seven miles beneath the mountain and powered by energy cleverly extracted "from the sun, the moon and the cosmic ray itself." However, these colonists according to Doreal were not Lemurians, but Atlanteans, and the colony at that time numbered 353, although he was told by his hosts that there were Lemurians who lived still deeper in the earth, who numbered approximately 4+ million."

Mt. Shasta is not only well-known for its mystical quality, but also has many other interesting aspects, and is noted for many reasons. It has been noted in the past to people in all parts of the world because of its famous mineral waters, which are believed to possess great healing and rejuvenating powers. To the aesthetic it is noted for its sublime beauty. To the theosophist it is still noted for its occult aspects. To the mountaineer and hiker, its lofty slopes offer interesting adventures, including a popular ski resort when one is in the mood to ski the perennial glaciers which embrace the sides of the mountain. And to many, the mountain has a deep, religious symbolic significance, so much so that it has been labeled by many as "The American Mecca". People come from all parts of the world to enjoy the Stewart Mineral Springs and baths, near the town of Weed, and the origin place of the "healing waters", as well as to view the annual "I AM" Activity pageant, a wonderfully presented depiction of the life of Christ. Another attraction is the Lake Shasta Caverns, located in O'Brien, California, about 13 miles north of Redding on I-5. Lake Shasta Caverns offers an interesting 3-part tour which takes one on a relaxing ferry ride across the lake on the aptly-named "Cavern Queen", followed by a breathtaking ride by bus up to the entrance of the cave, some 800 feet above the lake, followed by the cave trip itself, an experience worthy of all efforts to reach the cave. Towering above the surrounding hills, the resplendent snow-capped peaks of majestic Mt. Shasta are undeniably the most conspicuous and awesome natural landmark in the entire region of northern California, and in its solitary magnificence, mantled with perpetual snow and ice, it is indeed, the "Jewel of Siskiyou County."

Miller and Eichorn

To the early pioneer Mt. Shasta became a landmark which was eagerly sought, as if it were the end of a trail which promised many things. Even now, the many travelers by rail and highway, crane their necks in anticipation of the first view of this majestic mountain, which can be seen as far away as a hundred miles or more from certain vantage points. From the north the mountain may be seen through the distant haze from many points in southern Oregon, and it was from such a vantage point that the early explorer Joaquin Miller as a young man had his first sight of Mt. Shasta whereupon he immediately fell in love with the mountain. This "love at first sight" inspired him to writes "I uncover my head, and then turn my face to Mt. Shasta and kiss my hand, for want of a better expression."

Like many other observers, Joaquin Miller believed that Mt. Shasta was the most beautiful mountain of the west: "Mt. Hood is a magnificent idol, is sufficient, if you do not see Mt. Shasta." and adding his famous remarks "Lonely as God and white as a winter moon." Miller's assertion was later confirmed by an unknown author, who wrote the following words which are taken from some old travel brochures

"I have just crossed the Atlantic and the North American continent to see Mt. Shasta, and had I not been permitted to see anything else in all my journey, I would feel amply repaid with one day spent in the shadow of the grand old mountain, to see one glorious sunset when the last rays of light fall on the snowy crest changing in hue from golden to pink to purple, forming a picture too grand for any poet to describe, to beautiful for any artist to paint and leaving an impression on the mind never to be forgotten."

The early expert on Mt. Shasta, Arthur F. Eichorn, sums up this idea of Mt. Shasta's unearthly beauty in the following words: "To the serious student of occultism, Mt. Shasta is often called California's mystery mountain. For to see

Mt. Shasta on a bright moonlit night, especially in the early fall of the year, when the harvest moon casts its silver rays on the snow-mantled slopes, gleaming like molten silver, appearing like a ghostly tower, it is not too difficult to believe some of the fascinating stories that have persisted throughout the years regarding its occult aspects."

Who Discovered Mount Shasta?

It is officially recorded in the history of the Mount Shasta region that the mountain was "discovered" by a fur trader, one Peter Skene Ogden, on the winter day of February 14, 1827.

At the age of 17, in the year 1811, young Peter Skene Ogden entered the service of the North West Company at Montreal. Previous to this he was a law student, and prior to that for a short time, a clerk for one John Jacob Astor. He first came west to the state of Oregon in 1818 for the North West Company, his headquarters being at Fort George (Astoria).

While on a fur trading trip in the year 1827, Ogden passed through the valley to the northwest of Mt. Shasta, which is known today as Shasta Valley. At a place somewhere in the south of this valley he came upon a river. Here he paused and made the following notation in his diary made of beaver skins "All the Indians here persist they know nothing of the sea. I have named this river Sastise River. There is a mountain equal in height to Mt. Hood or Vancouver. I have named it Mount Sastise. I have given these names from the tribes of Indians." This historic notation was made by Ogden on February 14, 1827.

However, according to an old Spanish manuscript, Ogden may not have been the first white man to see the mountain, and that it may have been observed as early as 1817, which would seem to agree with the argument of some historians that such a conspicuous landmark could not have remained unseen until 1827, especially since other peaks such as Mts. Rainier, Hood, St. Helens, Baker, St. Elias, Popocatepetl—in fact, practically all the other great mountain masses of the Pacific Coast had been named and mapped before the beginning of the eighteenth century.

On May 20, 1817, a group of Spanish explorers under the leadership of Captain Luis Arguello, while ascending the Sacramento River paused to make camp at an undisclosed place. Duran, who was apparently the scribe of the expedition wrote: "At about ten leagues to the northwest of this place we saw the very high hill called by the soldiers that went near its slope Jesus Maria. It is entirely covered with snow. They say that a great river of the same name runs near it, and that it enters the Sacramento River, and they conjecture that it may be some branch of the Columbia. This I have heard from some soldiers; let the truth be what it may.'"

Other historians claim that Shasta may have been seen by white man earlier still, before the Spanish expedition up the Sacramento. They claim that the Russian settlers of the Bodego region may have seen the mountain, albeit at a considerable distance, as early as 1812, which was the year they founded Fort Ross. Regardless of the mystery of the mountain's original "discoverer", or of the mystery of the origin of it's name, Mt. Shasta stands today as if unconquerable, seemly defiant of all argument over it's past or destiny, for Shasta has stood long before America came into being and will probably stand for ages after the nations pass away.

The stories the Indians in the vicinity of Mt. Shasta tell are quite interesting. One legend states that long before the advent of man, the earth was populated by a race of animal people. In the mythology of the Indian, the Coyote was held in high esteem. He was the dominant leader of the animal kingdom because of his great wisdom and shrewdness.

In the legend of the great flood, which may have been the Indian's record of the sinking of Lemuria, the Coyote is said to have angered the Evil Spirit, and in retaliation the evil one made the waters rise until the land was covered, that is, all except the top of Mt. Shasta. Here on the summit the various animals sought refuge and remained until the waters receded. The animals then returned to the valleys and plains, and became the propagators of the animals of today.

The Little People and the Giants

Among the many legends originating from mysterious Shasta is that of the so-called "Little People." One of the many sites near Shasta where sightings of these curious little folk have been reported is known today as the "Siskiyou Stone Circles", a group of artifacts which have kept the archaeologists mystified and without any positive idea as to how they came to be, who built them, or for what purpose.

Umberto V. Orsi, writing in FATE Magazine in 1953, gives us the following answer to the mysterious enigma of the Stone Circles: "The Mysterious Circles of Shasta, better known as the Siskiyou Stone Circles, were made for a specific purpose. I believe I know what the circles are used for. They were made by the little people who live either beneath the surface of the surrounding terrain or within the mountain itself. There is no law, written or unwritten, that says people have to live upon a planet's surface. It is safer to dwell within a planet. These people are not the only inhabitants of this region. There are others too -- and I don't mean U.S. citizens, either. And they possess great knowledge which they use well."

Those who tend to be amused by the idea that outsized or diminutive species of man may have lived on earth in the past, or better yet to the present day, should be reminded of the already diversified races of man which are officially known to exist. These range from the very small pigmy races of some 3 feet in height to the well-known Watusi of Africa who often grow to heights of eight feet or more. In fact, Nature seems to take delight in creating many diversities within a single "family" of animals. Take for instance the cat family, which ranges from the small, harmless housecat on up to the fearsome Lord of the jungle, the Lion. This is also true with the lizard family, which has ranged in size from the small types which can easily be held in the palm of a man's hand to the gigantic, ancient lizard, the Ultrasaurus, which stood as tall as a five-story building. This can also be seen in the Sapien family, which ranges from the tiny spider monkeys small enough to wrap themselves around the finger of a man, to the large Gorilla. The same divergence is also true with other animal families - Dogs, Fish, Whales, Spiders, etc., who all come in a wide variety of sizes and features. Is it too impossible then to believe, considering the above facts, that Nature may have seen fit that man also evolve into a widely diversified family of different races, ranging as little as twelve inches to as much as twelve feet in height?

The Bible even refers to a giant race called the Nephilim (Gen. 6:4) as well as the giant Anikim, spoken of by Moses, a people so huge that he and his followers "were as grasshoppers in their sight" (Num. 13:33). In fact, the Bible seems to indicate that there were several such races of giant men who lived in pre-deluge times, and that many of these perished in the Flood (sinking of Lemuria?), not being allowed to enter the Ark.

One report of interest here was one which appeared in the Sunday, October 30, 1955 issue of THE SAN FRANCISCO EXAMINER. This issue carried a story with photographs which originated in the Siskiyou News, Yreka, California, proclaiming that a gigantic footprint with three toes was found on the slopes of Mt. Shasta. This footprint was found at the 11,000 foot level of the mountain by John W. Chamberlin, a Yreka newspaperman who was the leader at the time of an expedition seeking traces of the Lemurians in the Mt. Shasta area.

Other reports of very similar discoveries of the actual caves wherein the "Giant Lemurians" lived seem to support the believe that Lemuria did in fact harbor a race of Giants, and the added belief that the western part of North America was at one time joined with the ancient continent.

Encounters On The Mountain

There appeared several years ago a story of another man whose life was changed during a night he spent on the mountain. This particular individual, while out hiking in the mountain on a particularly cloudy day, noticed that it suddenly started to rain quite heavily. Seeking shelter beneath a nearby tree he eventually ly became drowsy and dozed off into a deep sleep. He awoke sometime during the night only to find that it was still raining, and noticed that he was covered in a warm blanket of some strange make, similar to a shagged carpet of artificial fur which appeared to be as soft and luxurious as the finest mink pelts. Being quite tired still, he didn't give it much thought and contented himself to fall back to sleep. In the morning he awoke to find that the strange blanket was gone. It wasn't until then that he realized the strangeness of his situation. Apparently someone had been there during the night and covered him with the blanket to keep him warm and dry. He left the mountain the next morning quite mystified, to say the least.

A famous mystery school called the ASTARA movement had its origin partly as the result of an experience which the founders Earlyne and Robert Chaney had on Mt. Shasta. After walking some distance up the mountain as they were instructed to do by the Master Teacher RAMA, a member of the spiritual Hierarchy and cosmic benefactor of the Astara Movement, with whom they were in contact, the Chaney's soon came to a halt. There standing before them was a handsome young mans

"I wish so much that I could say he was like a man from another world. I wish I could say he had long tresses and wore a flowing white robe and sandals," states Earlyne Chaney in her book SECRETS FROM MOUNT SHASTA, "that he resembled the mysterious lost Lemurians, the gods of antiquity, waiting to touch us with his rod of power and transform us instantly into radiant initiates. But I cannot.

"He was not unlike any other man one would meet on the street of any city. He had black hair and combed it straight back from his forehead. He wore a short-sleeved shirt, high at the throat. He wore white slacks and, ah, yes... there WAS something different! The belt he wore. It seemed to be made of old silver or pewter, interwoven with strands of leather. It was fairly wide, and carved on it were the signs of the zodiac.

"His arms were very brown, and about each wrist he wore wide, tight bracelets of the same substance as his belt, except that in the center of the pewter, prominently displayed on each bracelet, was the All-Seeing Eye. Later, on closer examination, we discovered that this Eye was made of some mysterious gem which had no color of its own, yet seemed to reflect the color of all things surrounding it, as a mirror or a clear crystal might do. On his feet he wore rubber-soled sandals..."

The "mysterious visitor" introduced himself as Idosa, whom they had reason to believe was a member of an ancient Brotherhood known as the Universal Order of Melchizedek, which according to information they received from the spiritual Hierarchy was "the Order of initiates which we knew to be existent not only on R throughout various planetary systems."

Home of the Underground Dwellers and Ancient Gods

After a short discourse on ancient mysteries and Cosmic doctrines, Idosa led the couple to a hidden cavern. They entered the cave, which they learned was named "The Cave of the Mystic Circle", and followed a series of tunnels to a place which concealed an entrance to another room. Upon entering this ceremonial room they encountered in its center a triangular stone slab, or digs, from one corner of which emerged a steady blue flame the origin of which they were unable to determine. This small flame gave off no heat or smoke, burning steadily without a flicker, and seemingly illuminating the entire rooms

"...This, he said, was the Lesser Temple, and it was here he came when he wished to retreat from the world. He told us there was an obscure door which led out of this Cave -- which he called the Cave of the Mystic Circle -- and said that behind that door would be found quite a comfortable place to bide awhile, although he did not even take us into those quarters. I glanced around, hoping to discern the door. I never did locate it. It was either very well concealed or it was one of those mysterious portals which opened by a secret Word or Power or touch -- like those in the pyramids and temples of Egypt.

"The Cave of the Mystic Circle was wholly bare save for the triangular slab of stone and the blue light. So we had not actually seen, nor were we to see, anything at all unusual there, in material substance, on top of Mount Shasta. Any wanderer might explore the outer Cave -- and even this inner Cave -- and still not obtain any secrets. If by chance he discovered this inner Cave, the triangle of stone would arouse his curiosity, but it would remain as silent as the Sphinx so far as revealing any mysteries."

The three of them at that time underwent a strange ceremony, during which they were raptured up in their Spirit bodies, and leaving their physical bodies behind they ascended the mountain, which appeared much different in this higher dimensional reality in which they found themselves. At the top of the mountain they came to a magnificent Cathedral beyond description. This of course, according to the Chaney's, was not visible in the mundane third dimension. Within this temple they underwent an Initiation by Fire and attended an awe-inspiring gathering of the Great Brotherhoods before returning to their physical bodies. As a reminder of their wonderful experience the Masters "apported" to them a beautiful five-pointed crystal which "radiates a remarkable power." Earlyne later had this crystal mounted in a golden amulet symbolically embodying the All-Seeing Eye and Seven-Pointed Star. The amulet was created to resemble as closely as possible two similar ones which were placed about their necks and over their hearts during the high point of their initiation high atop Mt. Shasta's etheric temple. This amulet is now worn often by Earlyne Chaney at Astara seminars all over the country, especially during her lectures and healing services.'

Lemurians and Native-Americans

As further evidence for the existence of Lemurian survivors, let us now quote from a Hokan-Siouan origin legend as it is related by Joseph H. Wherry in his INDIAN MASKS AND MYTHS OF THE WEST:

"In the dim and distant past the forebears of many of the California Indians lived on an island somewhere in the Western. This island was Elam and they worshiped the powerful god named Mu. Bear Mother was the mother of fifty daughters and the head of the people and she had large fields on other nearby islands where crops were tilled. It was the habit of the daughters and the people to go in their canoes to the island where they tilled their crops during the day. Every evening they returned to their village on Elam where Bear Mother watched over the fires in all of the dwellings while her clan was working..."

Yet another California tribe, now extinct from a plague of smallpox brought over by the white man, also claimed to have come from this same island, or continent, which they called Elam-Mu. They added that on this great island were a series of large man-made canals, which was represented' in their symbology by three concentric circles, one inside the other, intersected in the center by a vertical and horizontal line thus forming a cross. The end of this tribe came when a white man intentionally gave the chief of this tribe a "gift" blanket from a man who died from smallpox. Over 15,000 Indians died from the plague that followed. Joseph Wherry adds that the migration myths of the North-West and California "suggest an intriguing land somewhere in the Pacific Ocean where the 'first people' worshiped a high being named Mu. That this conjures a famous land of the same name is evident."

There are reports of another group of Lemurian descendants who lived in the islands off Santa Barbara several years ago, who were known as the "Chumash." The Chumash were one of a number of groups of tribes of separated communities who claimed to be direct descendants of the Lemurians. The Chumash, who numbered well over 35,000 when they were discovered by Cabrillo in 1654, quickly dwindled in number soon after the white man and the missionaries arrived in large numbers. In 1771 only 8,960 natives remained, and in 1900 three families consisting of nine adults remained, while thirty years later only one of these adults was living, and it is said that he was taken by his Lemurian brethren into another secret community.`'

Sydnay A. Clarm, in his book GOLDEN TAPESTRY OF CALIFORNIA sums up the mysteries of Mt. Shasta in the following words:

"...Mt. Shasta, as well as the city of that name, and Shasta Springs are curiously not in Shasta County at all but in Siskiyou County, which takes its name possibly from the Six Rocks (Six Caillous) which a pioneer French

Canadian guide used as a ford to cross the Umpqua River. No county, however, is big enough to monopolize this mountain, which can be seen from many counties round about, including one or two in Oregon. Its name is sometimes said to be derived from the Russian word Tschasta, meaning chaste, but however desirable and romantic this might be in tribute to its eternal mantle of pure white, it is incorrect, for the Indians bestowed the name upon it, and Peter Ogden, the Hudson's Bay trapper who first discovered it in 1826, merely borrowed the name already in use.

"There is an awesome air of mystery about Shasta with which few mountains seem able to clothe themselves, and this accounts, perhaps, for the unusual stories which are circulated, and often believed, about a strange village of Lemurians in a glen at the mountains base. The Lemurians are supposed to be descendants of that race which inhabited a prehistoric continent long since vanished beneath the waters of the Pacific. Individuals and groups are always hunting for this village and in the fall of 1930 a band of Rosicrucians came from Santa Cruz and spent some time in an organized search. One Frater Selvius wrote a long article about it in the Rosicrucian Digest of May, 1931. It discoursed at length on 'the strangest mystical village in the Western Hemisphere, where the last descendants of the ancient Lemurians, the first inhabitants of this earth, find seclusion, protection and peace. Various members of the community, in pure white, gray-haired, bare-foot and very tall have been seen on the highways and in the streets of the villages near Shasta. Many testify to having seen the strange boat, or boats, which sail the Pacific Ocean, and then rise at its shores and sail through the air to drop again in the vicinity of Shasta. This boat has neither sails nor smokestacks.'

"There is much more, but Mt. Shasta, being lost in lofty contemplation is likely to give little heed to the racial affiliations of those of those curious little creatures called men who make their home at its base..."

So without further introduction, let us now continue with the various personal accounts of Shasta as they are related by individuals who seem to share a common fascination for this magical monument of Nature.

Many of these accounts are incredible and a little hard to believe to say the least, especially to the skeptic, but I ask you to keep an open mind and remember that throughout the history of mankind, the impossible and improbable has had a strange way of making itself a reality or fact. Whether or not the following accounts prove in the long run to be true, or just the result of a series of overactive imaginations remains to be seen. I leave the reader to judge according to his or her own analysis of the evidence.

However, I am sure that many of you will agree that these separate accounts do seem to support each other. And who knows, perhaps one day when they feel that we are ready, the reticent inhabitants of Mt. Shasta, if they really do exist, might make themselves known to humankind and bring the mystery of Mt. Shasta to a close forever. If and when this does occur, let us hope that with their thousands of years of experience and superior knowledge, they will be able to teach us backward humans how to live without destroying ourselves by following in the footsteps of the ancient Atlanteans and other forgotten races who brought on their own destructions. Perhaps this time, with the help of the Lemurians, we will learn before it is too late.

Fig. 26 - Mount Shasta circa 1919

Fig. 27 - Mount Shasta Observer From the Summit of Mount Lassen

Fig. 28 - Mt Shasta by A.L. McBride

Fig. 29 - Frederick A. Butman (1821-1871), Mount Shasta

The Occult Connection

Mount Shasta—I Have Been There!

By Dr. Wendy Lockwood, Ph.D

Fig. 30 - Wendy Lockwood

Dr. Wendy Lockwood is a lifetime student of the otherworldly and the paranormal. The process began for her before birth; she came into the world with memories of former lives embedded within her, many of which she later verified in this lifetime through diligent research. She has studied under the esoteric icon and teacher Dr. M. Doreal and maintained a personal correspondence with Richard Shaver of the Inner Earth Mysteries.

To join a mailing list for Lockwood's "Web of Light Newsletter," send a check or money order for $25 for twelve issues to Dr. Wendy Lockwood, Ph.D., 31250 John Wallace Road, #102, Evergreen. CO, 80439.

There have been many erroneous claims written about Mt. Shasta. People are told that living in the inner mountain is a colony of Lemurians. That is absolutely not true.

Home of the Underground Dwellers and Ancient Gods

The late Dr. M. Doreal, one of the world's greatest Tibetan-trained Master-Gurus, myself, and many enlightened Masters have been there. Certain geologists and volcanologists claim that Shasta is a dormant volcano. In fact, it is totally extinct, being dead for almost 100,000 years.

Mt. Shasta is the home of Enlightened Atlantean Masters, a wondrous abode where only those who are sincere students, Master's Chelas, or Masters themselves may enter by invitation only. It is not a place for the seeker of phenomena or unique thrills, but a place of the highest education, far beyond our mundane universities, into ancient advanced sciences, such as quantum metaphysics and pre-deluvian high tech, light years ahead of our present primitive, fossil fuel and electronic era.

Within the seven-mile deep heart of Mt. Shasta, dwell the keepers of the ancient archives, machines and devices, not even dreamed of today. "Extinct" flora, fauna and a might cigar-spaceship that exits the mountain every month to fly over the ocean toward the South Pacific to inspect the locks on the Caroline islands where the rebellious Lemurians are held prisoner. The natives on those islands whisper about fearful, haunting phenomena and chanting on the island of Nan-Madol during the full moon.

On Nan-Madol, are colossal temple ruins which clearly belonged to an advanced race. Occasionally the Lemurians break through to the surface and the Shasta ship must re-seal those tunnels because they are a very serious danger to surface civilizations. The worst criminals here compare to the best of the Lemurians.

That hollow, or space was formed after the great global conflict with Atlantis. The Atlantean Masters used nuclear weapons on the Lemurians because they sought to take over and enslave the world, being extremely diabolical.

Through ancient high technology, the Great Masters drew a mighty mass of that Lemurian continent out of the sea, sealing the hollow over and casting it into orbit around our Earth. This is now known as the Moon. The craters on the Moon are not meteor craters; they are scars from mighty warfare between the survivors on the Moon and the Atlantean Masters. The Moon is a child of the Earth, and the moon rocks retrieved by the astronauts are very much like sand and basalt from the South Pacific.

The Lemurians were controlled by the Reptilians, who previously invaded Earth from the shattered planet Eros, now the asteroid belt between Mars and Jupiter. They have the ability to morph, or throw an illusion around themselves to appear as human. Their true appearance somewhat resembles ET of the movie, which was meant to make children receptive to the reptoids because children are easily misled.

Those Reptilians are diabolically immoral and possess a method by which they can take-over, usually a famous person's body, or someone in a position of "trust," such as schools, lodges, charities, the media, religion, celebrities and some royalty, as well as politicians. Occasionally those in disguise are sometimes revealed by their snake-eyes, which break through the illusion.

I have already seen several "charming" leaders with snake-eyes because many of those ancient reptilians still strive to deceive and enslave the world under global dictatorship. They aspire to take-over all nations under the pretense of liberal change and false promise.

Again, remember, Mt. Shasta powerfully relates to the age-old conflict. I do not speak or write from theory, folklore, legend, theology or borrowed concepts, but from my own experiences and from my truth-vowed teachers and gurus.

The Lemurians worshipped three gods: the sun god, the moon god and the reptilian god. The reptoid-beings antedated both Atlantis and Lemuria. Lemuria sank before Atlantis, and Atlantis sank due to Lemurian invaders and the polar shift. Because of these events, the Earth was totally devastated.

Just prior to the sinking of Atlantis, the priest-king Masters and their Chelus fled to Mt. Shasta. For many years they had prepared the mountain as a place of refuge, and when Atlantis was invaded by the Lemurian reptoids the Masters descended to the pyramid of balance in the inner earth and tilted Earth on its axis, in an attempt to halt the reptilian invasion.

A Visit To Mt. Shasta

In 1932, Dr. Doreal was first invited to Mt. Shasta by two men who met him at a class he was lecturing at in Hollywood. I have also been taken to Mt. Shasta under similar circumstances, the first time with two escorts. At that time my husband worked the night shift as communications manager for the local railroad station in Stockton, California and I was often alone with just my toddler son.

That night I retired early, only to awaken to the voices of two men repeating: "Come on Wendy, sit-up." I had no fear, and as I sat up, they placed a belt-like device around my waist and a clear mask over my face.

Taking my hands, we arose up through the ceiling and out into the star-studded velvet vault of the summer night. Northward we flew at a very high velocity, but I felt very little movement. Below us the lights of the cities and towns blurred. In minutes, there before us loomed the vast, beautiful summit of the 14,000 foot Mt. Shasta, glowing in the moonlight.

We set down on a flat stone area upon its highest peak. Then the rock began to silently descend down a tubular shaft, deep into the core of the mountain.

I stopped at an arched opening looking out across an enormous paradise contained within a cavern so large that we could not see the walls. To our right was a beautiful white temple, and ahead of us spread thousands of acres of rolling, forested hills that faded into the mists. The cavern is plush with rare and "extinct" flora and fauna.

Under the opalescent rays of an artificial sun, millions of colorful birds sang in great symphonies that echoed in the fragrant golden atmosphere. The deadly rays from that sun are released through vents on the mountain top, leading scientists to believe that Mt. Shasta still has a fiery life buried deep within the planet.

Twenty Secret Cities That Lead To Shasta

Where I now live, here in the Colorado Rockies, only a short distance below is one of the twenty secret cities of the White Lodge which leads to Mt. Shasta. Several times I have bi-located there. (We know it is bi-location because material beings see and relate to us.)

It is a wonderful place where the beautiful, eyeless Blue Race dwells. They are our best friends and are preparing a refuge for the peace-loving, positive people who will be separated from the great Earth changes and chaotic surface conditions which will involve the axis shift, global war, extreme weather, quakes, fires, winds and floods.

Global warming is a natural part of those great corrective changes. Beneath the ice caps will be discovered ancient cities and fantastic technologies from eons ago.

The caves of the lesser cities of Shamballa are all surrounded by 9th dimensional space warps, so when Mother Earth suffers her global seizures, nothing will touch those twenty subterranean sacred cities of the White Lodge. The small city near where I live here in Evergreen, Colorado, has many annexed caverns, some so enormous that they are like separate worlds, and there are huge vegetable and fruit gardens extending for great distances, each having enormous fruits and vegetables.

I was escorted by a lovely eyeless, blue-skinned lady with white hair who was able to see through her third eye. She wore a robe that sparkled with golden mesh over it. She led me into a large, brightly lit cavern with several entrances. In long rows sat tables with deep edgings filled with gigantic fruits and vegetables.

Reaching over and patting a giant, divinely fragrant, velvet covered peach, she asked, "How old do you think this peach is?"

I quickly replied, "Oh, perhaps under a week old."

She smiled and answered, "It is 100 years old and is as fresh as the day it was picked."

She then led me to vast apple orchards; mostly the golden delicious variety, all were as large as the peach. One dare not stand beneath such trees.

On another visit I was shown a great semi-darkened cave with smooth polished floors and mountains of boxes full of survival gear. Each box is coated with a shiny black substance to keep their contents perfectly preserved for the day that they will be needed.

The main cavern resembles the Shasta cavern, only smaller. Shasta has two large caverns atop each other. The main Shasta cavern is twenty miles across and two miles deep. The one near my home has its own suspended, artificial sun and is about seven miles long, two miles wide and a couple of miles deep.

All the twelve secret cities located around the world are in caverns with man-made suns and a golden, fragrant atmosphere. They are full of enormous, harmless, insects and butterflies with 30-inch wingspans.

On another Mt. Shasta visit, I was taken on a levitated flight over the cavern terrain in a small colorful, open-topped shuttle that resembled a carnival bumper car. The cavern walls are grooved to serve as drains for the terrarium-like moisture to drain back into the creeks and soil.

On another visit to the Colorado cave-city, I was shown their anti-gravity vehicles that are mostly used for leisure. They are colorful, spherical vessels with a full glass dome on the upper half and solid quarters below. Encircling the upper dome portion is a built-in sofa. In the center of the floor descends a staircase to the concealed lower spaces, with an exit at the base.

I was then led to a great pillared arched entrance to a wide boulevard that exited the city on the west-side. Ahead, the highway tunnel vanished to a point in the distance. Along the sides of the corridor were parked attractive, colorful shuttle cars like those in Mt. Shasta. Each car sat in place, levitating about six or seven inches off the surface. I was invited to step into it by the lady who was my host, and it softly floated up and down as I took my seat.

Suddenly, without sensation, we were moving through the tunnel at a very high speed. We then slowed down for a while and here and there along the way other tunnels merged or branched off.

After what seemed to be about fifteen minutes, we slowed down at a check station which was directly below Mt. Shasta (about 1500 miles from Colorado). We were questioned and screened to see if we qualified to enter the mountain. We were then let through.

I was taken to a very large cavern, joining several other students. We were told that Mt. Shasta was a cosmic university where advanced students are and will be taught directly from the Atlantean archives. These students are being taught in preparation for the great changes that will soon befall planet Earth and the coming of a great teacher who will lead the survivors out of the darkness and into the light of supreme consciousness.

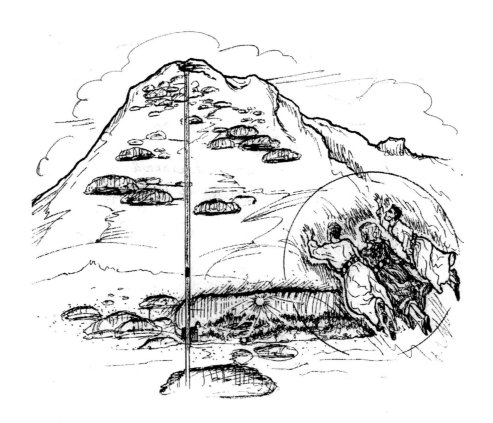

Before us loomed the vast, beautiful summit of the 14,000 foot Mt. Shasta, glowing in the moonlight.

Fig. 31 -Drawing of the Mystical Mount Shasta

World Teacher Will Emerge From Mt. Shasta

Mt. Shasta is also connected to the hollow Earth through the world-wide network of secret tunnels. I have been in that exquisite land beneath our feet, and there are truly no worlds to express its beauty. The rays of the inner sun (called "They Abyss") reach out through the polar openings to create the northern lights.

From this beautiful inner world dwells Harjas, the Pleiadean World Teacher. Harjas will emerge through Mt. Shasta after the great changes convulse the surface would and send humankind fleeing for their lives.

Harjas will be accompanied by his armies of rescue and honor to begin the repair of our devastated world; again establishing America as the first Cosmic Central School of the World. Mankind will have to radically alter his understanding and knowledge of science because he often errors, especially about self and his comprehension of astronomy and the world.

On July 18, 2007, as I sat in meditation, a great figure, about ten feet tall, walked through my door, stooping to enter the room. Immediately I recognized his as Harjas, as I had met him before. This time, however, instead of the ceremonial robes, he wore only a blue and white striped tee-shirt, blue jeans and white sneakers.

He had curly blond hair and blue eyes and is the ideal personification of a humanized God. Walking over to my right side, he held his right hand over my head where my crown chakra is. He directed energies into my third eye from his hand and I felt a powerful force filling my very being.

Mt. Shasta will be his gateway to the world after the Earth changes, and all will see as I have seen. The Mt. Shasta mystery is absolutely real and will soon be opened to all in the years ahead.

Fig. 32 - Gilbert Munger (1863-1903), Mount Shasta

Fig. 33 - John J. Young (1830-1879), Shasta Butte and Shasta Valley

Fig. 34 - Eugene Camerer (1830-1898), Shasta Butte and Shasta Valley

The Metaphysical-- Spiritual Realm

MAJESTIC SHASTA — ENTRY POINT OF THE LIGHT GRIDS

AN INCREDIBLE JOURNEY TO ANOTHER DIMENSION

THE STARDOVES TRANSFORMATION PROPHECIES

Fig. 35- Earl Lamb (1889-1984). Timber wolves and Mount Shasta

Fig. 36- Cleveland Rockwell (1837-1907), Mount Shasta

The Metaphysical * Spiritual Realm

Majestic Shasta—Entry Point Of The Light Grids

By Yvonne Moore

For the past ten years, Yvonne, known as Zadessa (the name she was given when she channels) to the inter-dimensional space beings and to her colleagues Yashah and Dr. Ki, has been the photographer for Alahoy Books. Yvonne accompanied Yashah and Dr. Ki on many UFO sightings throughout British Columbia and also during numerous trips to Washington, Oregon and Mount Shasta, California. These sightings occurred at vortex locations.

Yvonne always had her video camera at her side and was always eager to snap pictures. She has video and other camera pictures of UFOs in flight as well as other inter-dimensional phenomena.

Yvonne lives smack in the middle of the Surrey Corridor in British Columbia. More information can be found at her website at:

http://modena.intergate.ca/personal/alahoy/page2.htm

What follows here is Yvonne's overview of some of the history and myth that has grown up around Mount Shasta.

Mt. Shasta is a most majestic mountain located at the northern extremity of the Sierra Nevada Mountains of Siskiyou County in Northern California about 35 miles from the Oregon border. Mt. Shasta is the core of an extinct volcano raising a height of 14,162 feet above sea level, and it the largest volcanic peak in the continental United States.

Mt. Shasta is very special to say the least. It represents much more than just a mere mountain. Mt. Shasta can be considered as one of the most sacred places on the planet. It is a focus for angels, spirit guides and masters from the realms and home survivors which sank under the Pacific Ocean a little over 12,000 years ago. For those with clairvoyant abilities, Mt. Shasta is embraced in a gigantic etheric pyramid whose capstone reaches far beyond this planet into space and connects us inter- galactically to the Confederation of Planets for this sector of the 'Milky Way Galaxy.' This pyramid is also created as an inversion of itself, reaching down to the very core of the Earth.

Mt. Shasta is the entry point of the light grids of this planet, where most of the energy comes first from galactic and universal cores. It is disseminated to other mountains to and into other grids, most mountains tops, especially the tall mountains are Beacons of Light feeding the light-grids of this planet, where most of the energy comes from first, from the galactic and universal core. It is disseminated to other mountains and into the grids.

Strange lights and sounds are often seen and heard on the mountain. Spacecraft drowned in layers of clouds, shadows and outstanding sunsets add to the aura of the mountain. Several tunnels stretch far into the interior of this majestic mountain. Mt. Shasta is the home of the present-day Lemurians, survivor of the sinking continent of Mu over 12,000 years ago. Yes, our Lemurian brothers and sisters are real, they are physically alive, living in the subterranean city of 'Telos' underneath Mt. Shasta.

Prior to the sinking of their continent, fully aware of the eventual destiny of their beloved continent the ancient Lemurians using mastery of energy, crystals, sound and vibrations, got their beloved city out of a vast underground city. Their treasures and their records of the ancient Earth's history has been lost since the sinking of Atlantis. Lemuria was once a vast continent, larger than the Americas, connected to parts of California, Oregon, Nevada and Washington.

The large continent disappeared over night into the Pacific Ocean over 12,000 years ago in a vast cataclysm. All people of he Earth at the time considered Lemuria in the land of Mu their motherland and there was much weeping on the Earth when that happened. About 25,000 Lemurians at the time were able to migrate to into the interior of Mt. Shasta. The most important of their various administrative centers prior to the sinking of the Motherland was saved. And Beloveds, as you are reading this writing, know in your heart that they have not left. They are still here in tangible physical, immortal bodies, totally unlimited in life of pure Heaven on Earth.

American Indians believed that Mt. Shasta was of such immense grandeur, that its existence could only be attributed to the creation of the "Great Spirit'. They also believed that an invisible core of little people about 4 feet tall, lived its slopes as Guardians often referred to as "The little people of Mt. Shasta' also kind of physical, but not quite, and they very often are seen visually around the mountain. They are third dimensional beings like the humans but they live on a slightly higher level of the third dimension, such as one and a half level, and they have the ability to make the residues visible and invisible at will. The reason they are not showing themselves physically to many people is because they have a collective fear of humans.

At one time they were as physical as we are and could not make themselves invisible at all. They were humans living at a time viciously themselves. They became so fearful of humans that they collectively asked the spiritual hierarchy they could of the planet for the dispensation to be elevated to be in their frequency so that they could make themselves invisible at will, in order to be able to continue their evolution.

There are reports of the Bigfoot race of people being seen on remote areas of Mt. Shasta, along with other mysterious beings. The Bigfoot people are now very few in numbers around the world and around Mt. Shasta. They are of an average intelligence and a peaceful heart. They have also obtained to be able to avoid confrontation with us, and thus, like the little people, avoid being harmed, mutilated and used as a slave race.

But for hundreds of thousands years humans have taken over arrogantly thinking that they have the right to control and manipulate other kingdoms that appear to be more vulnerable than they. Many of the species of the animal kingdom are physically with us always, and loved and honored by humans.

Dr. M. Doreal claimed years ago that he visited the Lemurians inside the mountain. He said that the space they came into was about 2 miles in height and about 20 miles long and 15 miles wide. He wrote that the light inside was as bright as a summer day. He became suspended almost in the center of a giant mass glowing of light. Another man reported that he fell asleep on Mt. Shasta, to be awakened by a Lemurian who led him to his cave which was paved with gold. The Lemurian told the man that there were a series of tunnels by a volcano that was under the earth like freeways - a world within a world.

The Lemurians have supposedly mastered atomic energy, telepathy and clairvovyant skills electronic and science as long as 18,000 years ago. They have technology that makes us surface dwellers look as toddlers compared to them. Back then they knew how to propel boats using energy radiated by crystals. They had airships and flew them to Atlantis and other places. Today they have a whole fleet with which come in and out of the mountain and into space. They also have the ability to make their space ships from being detected by the local and national military.

Just ever so often another mysterious story surfaces, new casts of characters emerge and attention is centered "once more a mystic mountain." That's the way it has been for years and perhaps always will be. Mt. Shasta has a tendency to reveal 'herseII7 only to those who honor life, honor themselves, who they truly are, honor the Earth, and honor all the kingdoms sharing this planet.

Though they are third dimensional people in nature, they are able to shift their energy field into fourth and fifth dimension and become invisible all within seconds. Many people report seeing strange lights on the mountain. One explanation is that there are spacecrafts coming and going constancy from a spaceport deep within the mountains. Mt. Shasta is not only home for the

Lemurians, but it is also an inter-planetary and inter-galactic multi-dimensionality portal. There is a huge etheric City of Light above Mt. Shasta called the Crystal City of the Seven Rays.

At some point, in our near future, hopefully within the next 12-20 years, this wonderful City of Light is to be lowered into our physical realm and become the first to manifest tangibly onto the planet. In order for this to happen, the people who live there will have to notch this vibration in their consciousness.

Many people report seeing strange lights on the mountain. One explanation is that spacecrafts are coming and going constantly from a spaceport deep within the mountains. Mt. Shasta is not only a home for the Lemurians, but it is also inter-planetary and inter-galactic multi-dimensionality portal.

You can easily visit Mt. Shasta without reading, but if you have formed connections with them you may be blessed with some new revelations. Mt. Shasta draws people from the world, some seeking spiritual insight, others seeking to query in the beauty and natural wonders that "Mother Nature' has to offer here in this unique alpine region.

Things have not changed so much on Earth in our days. We have not, as a species, understood that we are guests on this planet. Mother Earth has volunteered to provide a platform of evolution.

Fig. 37 - Robert Swain Gifford (1840-1905), Mount Shasta

Fig. 38 - Mount Shasta a Major Tourist Site and Resort

Fig. 39 -Frederick Ferdinand Schafer (1839-1927) Shasta & Full Moon

The Metaphysical * Spiritual Realm

An Incredible Journey Into The Other World of Mount Shasta

By Diane Tessman

*Ruth Montgomery's spirit guide, speaking in her book **Aliens Among Us**, said of Diane Tessman, "Space people are indeed able to contact through mental telepathy those who are open to their vibrations and take time for meditation, which is the only way to hear unspoken words. Diane's contact is real."*

With that endorsement from "the other side," one is not prone to doubt that Diane and her spirit guide Tibus are the genuine article. Diane has also served as a MUFON (Mutual UFO Network) state section director on the path to her current state of enlightenment and spiritual "readiness." She has been in contact with Tibus and other friendly entities since her early childhood. What follows here are Diane and Tibus' thoughts and feelings regarding some of the mysteries of Mount Shasta.

A myriad of magical, mystical and magnificent portals connect other dimensions to our daily reality all across our Mother Planet. These are sacred mountains, holy wells, special power spots within forests and deserts, beside mighty rivers and oceans, and in flowering meadows.

Dimensional portals exist in all climates and terrain, but they always touch us spiritually and psychically as we stand in awe of their energies. They also give us astounding paranormal experiences and profound spiritual visions. They hold ancient secrets, but also the promise of a new dawn for this poor old planet of ours.

Among these portals, Mount Shasta is among the most powerful. She is also a huge portal in sheer area, because the entire mountain of Shasta abounds with other-worldly consciousness, not just one small area.

My spirit guide, Tibus, who is with me as I write these words, insists that I call Mount Shasta "she," not "it."

Tibus says, "The energy of Gaia, the living spirit of Mother Earth, flourishes on outer slopes of Mount Shasta and within the inner sanctum of Mount Shasta.

The mountain herself is a living being. Her persona is feminine. When she speaks to us telepathically, she speaks in a musical female voice. She is a Mother Mountain and does not wish to be called 'it.'"

Tibus gives us the following message from the holy mountain herself:

Come, allow me to enfold you in my mystical arms if you come in peace, respecting and loving Mother Gaia. You will be safe within me but you will have an experience you will never forget, and you will gain new mystical knowledge, wisdom and power. You will not be the same after you have come to me, you will be more. Do not be frightened, for fear is the enemy of us all. I wish to communicate again, at the close of this chapter.

Long before Kenneth Arnold spotted the first "flying saucers" over Mount Ranier in 1947, people were seeing craft which were not of this world, flying into and out of Mount Shasta. Mount Rainier is a sister mountain of Shasta, and we understand that there are corridors which run between them. These are used by Inner Earth Dwellers in particular. We will speak more of this in a moment also.

For thousands of years, Native Americans have known Mount Shasta to be sacred and magical; Indians witnessed spirits fly in and out of Mount Shasta, especially at The Dark (of the moon) and The Full Moon.

Mount Shasta begs the question which also applies to other dimensional portals: Is she a "nuts and bolts" base for extraterrestrials? Do they have a base within this mountain which can be reached in our daily reality, if only we could find the entrance point and then make it safely to their city, deep inside the mountain? Have these space aliens, or human time travelers, been hiding inside Shasta for hundreds or perhaps thousands of years?

If this is so, their base deep within Mount Shasta is a place we can see, touch and experience within our frame of reality.

Or does Mount Shasta hold incredible buildings, bases and even cities in an other-dimensional reality? We might witness star craft (UFOs) and even living spirits zooming into and out of Shasta because the entire terrain of the mighty mountain herself is the dimensional access-portal!

In my years of metaphysical studies, and with my guide Tibus in agreement, we feel the second premise is true. Mount Shasta herself is magical!

The entire magnificent mountain exists in *two worlds!*

If you could travel through her dimensional portal, there she would be, just as she is in this world!

Tibus affirms that Shasta's dimensional portals can take you to a number of other dimensions. Some of these are fragment-worlds which are not complete realities. Her portals could even be used by a person who was spiritually ill, to reach negative, frightening places in the universe.

However, the Other-Dimensional Shasta, which looks exactly like Mount Shasta in our daily reality, is of a *higher* dimension. In fact, almost any of the many dimensions to which her portal can lead you are *positive higher realms.*

Mount Shasta is a powerful being who directly reflects the living spirit called Gaia, who is our Mother. Mother Planet Earth has both light and dark, miracles and disasters, but who can doubt that she is the wondrous creator of life! She is our mother, and the mother of all life forms on our orb. She is ultimately of The Light.

Who would we meet if we slipped through Shasta's portal and found ourselves on what looked like the same spot on the same mountain? Ah, but now we are on Shasta's twin-being. We call this twin flame, Other Dimensional Shasta.

This is exactly what happened to Earlyne and Robert Chaney on August 10, 1952. The Chaneys were the founders and leaders of Astara, the highly regarded metaphysical group. Both Chaneys have now passed on, and we have no doubt but what they are reveling in "the ethers of the Age of Aquarius," as they put it. My guide Tibus calls it The New Dawn of Earth.

In 1953, Earlyne wrote **Secrets From Mount Shasta**, which details the Chaneys' climb up Mount Shasta in search of spiritual truth and wisdom. At some point, Mount Shasta enfolded them in her arms, and they slipped onto the slopes of Other-Dimensional Shasta. This is not exactly the way Earlyne defined it, but it is Tibus' explanation of what happened.

The same magical encounter has happened to numbers of individuals, including Native Americans, for thousands of years before the white man arrived. The Chaneys had a long and dramatic encounter with the Other-Dimensional Shasta, perhaps because they were accomplished metaphysicians even in 1952, and so no fear entered into their experience.

Here are a few highlights of Earlyne's account:

" . . . I saw, with astral eyes, incredible, beautiful astral temples. Idosa (their guide for this experience) explained that "there are astral retreats deep within the heart of the mountain."

"My awareness stabilized in ever-expanding consciousness. I wore a gown of the most exquisite gossamer 'cobweb.' It floated like a vaporous cloud about me."

Earlyne looked to find her husband Robert in a "cassock robe," similar to Idosa's. Incidentally, Idosa had manifested on the mountainside just as the Chaneys slipped onto Other-Dimensional Shasta.

The Chaneys also encountered Egyptian Priest-King Zoser and "the touch of his hand was like a charge of high voltage electricity," Earlyne remembered. "The current swept from my head to my feet and rippled outward from me like an etheric tidal wave."

Earlyne gives fascinating insights into the world of Other-Dimensional Shasta. She states, "The Astral Cathedral sits directly over the Great Temple, at the peak of Mount Shasta. The Cathedral covers the entire peak of the Mount. Its brilliance so dazzled me that I had to temporarily avert my eyes. It shone as if it were made of innumerable diamonds, all flashing in the midday sun, except there was no sun. The dome of the Temple rose high, high into the sky. And there, over the dome, rising higher into the sky, was a glittering Star, which revolved around and around, very slowly, as a beacon of light does here on the Earth plane."

Today, 50-plus years after the Chaneys incredible journey, those who live near Mount Shasta observe the dazzling lights going into and out of the mighty mountain. Many of those who live near Mount Shasta are spiritual seekers and accomplished metaphysicians who still have incredible encounters with Other-Dimensional Shasta, her temples, her cathedrals and her advanced beings. People travel from around the world to experience Mount Shasta; she is indeed one of the most powerful portals on the face of the planet.

Tibus wishes us to look into one remaining question: Mount Shasta is home to etheric astral beings and their temples, and it is also a base for extraterrestrials and human time travelers, both of whom travel inter-dimensionally. But what about the Inner Earth Dwellers of Telos and other Inner Earth destinations? Are they the same as the Chaneys' astral beings, or are Inner Earth Dwellers of the Fairy Realm? Or are they of yet another dimension?

Tibus gives this input: "When one lives in the daily reality, it is difficult to imagine all the other dimensions which are out there, and which are within as well. I mean, within each of us, but also within our Mother, the Earth. But of course this is true, because we reflect her, she is our Source.

"We of other dimensions, which are of higher consciousness than your world, can travel between a myriad of dimensions. Extraterrestrials communicate with and work with Inner Earth Dwellers, for instance.

"The Chaneys Astral World of the Other-Shasta communicates with and works with Inner Earth Dwellers. We human time travelers (from Earth's future), communicate and work with all of these realms. We also know and love the beings of the Fairy and Angelic Realms.

Home of the Underground Dwellers and Ancient Gods

"It is a big Universe out there, and Mother Earth reflects this. She has created more dimensions and beings within these dimensions than can ever be imagined. So, to answer your question, Inner Earth Dwellers live deep within Other-Dimensional Earth. They may manifest from time to time in Mount Shasta's Astral Kingdom, but to be precise, these are two different dimensions. However, they know and love each other. They are cousins, you might say.

"Here's the thing: Once humankind transcends into The New Dawn of Earth, you will be able to see, interact with, learn from, and love positive beings from many, many dimensions. As long as you have not yet graduated spiritually, you are locked into the very limited reality of daily life. Your mind filters out everything it cannot understand.

"However, soon your spirit will overcome the chains of the mind, and you will soar with us, into the infinite and beautiful dimensions of the higher realms. No war ever, no money needed, no greed, no cruelty. You will love and care for your Mother Planet, not destroy her. Yes, it is possible and it is soon to be, because *I am of your future. You made it!*"

This is Mount Shasta's promise, too. Here is her closing message:

I long to live in a world where humans have learned to treasure and protect our Mother Creator. She is our Home World, unique and among the most vibrant in the whole Universe. I long for a time when my physical being will be in a spiritually evolved reality, just as my astral being is now. I long to enfold all enlightened humans in my mystical arms, because I love you just as much as I love my ET visitors, my Astral Kings and Queens, my Inner Earth Brothers and Sisters and my Future Human Friends.

I am a portal into The New Dawn of Earth. Of all my corridors to other realities, this is the most important. It is urgent, because Mother Earth is dying in the daily reality. Humankind has seen to this with its negligence and cruelty. My portal to The New Dawn offers salvation to humankind, because if you will only enlighten yourself, Earth will live in all dimensions, and so will you.

You must undergo the spiritual transformation of enlightenment. Turn away from war, from greed, from violence. NOW is the time to do it; the Point of Change approaches. We welcome you. The whole Universe will sing and celebrate your Graduation, and all the dimensions within my mighty mountain beinghood will rejoice!

You can write to Diane Tessman and receive a packet of free information! Write to Diane at P.O. Box 352, St. Ansgar, Iowa, 50472.

Email Diane at: dtessman@iowatelecom.net
Diane's website: dianetessman.com

Fig. 40 - Diane Tessman channels the being Tibus
who has drawn upon the energy of Mount Shasta

Fig. 41 - Henry Nappenbach (1862-1931) Shasta, the Grand Old Mountain
Changes the Schedule on the Oregon Line
(Notice the Face in the Mount Shasta?)

The Metaphysical * Spiritual Realm

The Stardoves Transformation Prophecies

By Stardoves
Dr. RAJa Merk Dove and
Prof. MoiRA Lady of the Sun Dove

As most of you know, Stardoves, Interdimensional Ambassadors of Light, www.stardoves.com, were recently deployed to Mount Shasta. Having physically led thousands throughout the world, to many sacred sites of Mother Earth, during their pilgrimages to India, Egypt, Mexico, the Philippines, Hawaii, Central America, Greece, Glastonbury, Palenque, Tibet, Nepal (and more), performing sacred Interdimensional Light Services, with the Council of 12. They have been brought to the Earth, to the star portals here in Mount Shasta for the purpose of cleansing and awakening gateways and providing outer support and a physical land base for all of these forces to be facilitated smoothly and efficiently. In this manner, Mother Earth may advance and have her 2,000 years of peace and harmony, basking in milk and honey but not "through the sweat of thy brow"!

As soon as Stardoves arrived at Mount Shasta and put out that message via these Internet Broadcasts, a message from Larry Frank came in, stating that according to various sources that remnants from the "lost" continent of Lemuria were able to escape the destruction of their continent by reportedly being able to relocate 25,000 survivors to an enormous cavern that is located beneath Mount Shasta. As many of you know, this is connected to other subterranean and "Hollow Earth" "Cities of Light," which Kiara Windrider wrote about in his book "Doorway to Eternity."

These survivors of Lemuria call their new home Telos, which means "Communication with Spirit." From this communication with "Spirit" they have created a highly evolved civilization where perpetual peace and joy exists for all, in a "world" in which they do not experience disease, aging (past 35) or death (by degeneration) of their physical bodies.

Larry brought to the attention of Stardoves that these survivors of Lemuria "have reportedly announced that they would like to emerge, in the very near future, to the surface and introduce themselves to their 'upstairs' neighbors who would welcome them."

Fig. 42 - Left: The Doves relax at home - Right: The Doves (Peace Ambassadors)

Eventually Larry sent to Stardoves two cassette tapes by International Channel Sophia On Ra. It was astounding how this channel recognized the Telosian Portal here and advised the McClung's about its location and that it needed to be moved to another area by trained clairvoyants and healers experienced in portal clearing service. On the tape, too, was Lady Jane McClung's observation of the portal as follows:

"It is a well-known fact that living next to Black Butte was like bathing in a very hot spa where all kinds of people were attracted to take a dip, and immediately whatever is inside, that being which did not serve the Highest Light was brought out to the surface, negatively affecting everyone around!" To which Sophia on Ra commented, "Indeed! For Black Butte is the heat vent for Mount Shasta!"

Stardoves now know very well, as does Adama, that we were preyed upon by negative forces masquerading in human bodies while in Taos. And, even here at this sacred Mount Shasta portal, negative forces gather to prevent us from going forth with the work the Masters have assigned us! It is such a strange mission here on Earth! Because of our actual experiences here for the past two months, we are beginning to totally rethink our strategy and location. We have learned that the entire area from Stewart Springs (northwest of Mount Shasta), including Mount Shasta to Big Bend Hot Springs to Mount Lassen, are actually what make up this entire megalithic sacred site that includes Inter-Dimensional Doorways, Inter-Galactic StarGates, Telosian Portals and Inner Retreat of the Ascended Masters, as well as where Shambhalla is relocating its Headquarters for the Spiritual Hierarchy of this planet for this Age and Dispensation.

Coming here was also a direct result of our contact with Adama and other Spiritual Masters assisting the Earth from the Stars. The focus was to take place at here at the home of the McClung's, where we are now blessed to have a refuge to do the work until we rebuild our Ashram here in Mount Shasta. Here we recognized this place immediately as a portal and a sacred site. Here is the beginning part of that work.

One startling piece of sacred information that Larry Frank shared with us that really piqued our interest is as follows: He told us that he noticed that an Inner Earth Being named Rosalea, who was his twin flame, just happens to nearly match our dear Moi-Ra's (a co-Stardove) biological earth name, which is Rosalia! Moi-Ra's connection to Lemuria (being from the Philippines) is accentuated now with her namesake being here underneath Mount Shasta, and this brings much hope and excitement! This following excerpt from Kiara's book sums up the type of energy that will allow one's access to the Portals: "Will we meet people we can trust? People whose hearts are open to us?"

Kryon Live Channeling, Mt. Shasta

JUNE 21-22 2003

Greetings, dear ones, I am Kryon on Magnetic Service. The energy is strong here.

Honoring those who are part of Mount Shasta.

It's time to speak of this area, Mount Shasta. There's no better time to speak of an area than when you're sitting in it, and it has much to do with the planet as a whole. It has a great deal to do with those reading this. Let's start with those who live here. I'd like to greet and celebrate the Guardians. This is a name we're giving to those who have vibrated higher almost all of their lives. They were born with the Lemurian energy, they could hardly wait to get here to Shasta. This is where they were drawn, and this is where they stayed.

They literally nursed the information of the mountain, the Guardians did. You might say they were the forerunners of the Lightworkers. But oh, they're more than that. They anchored and held the energy and kept it fresh around this mountain. It's fresh to this day! First-timers to the area: Are you aware of the kind of energy you walk within? Those of you who have trekked up the mountain know that it speaks to you. Did that surprise you? There's much going on here, and we're going to even rename the process.

The Guardians—who are they? They're the Human Beings who've lived in this mountain area for years and years and years. They've watched the comings and the goings—they've watched all the energy around the mountain—they've seen the truth and they've seen the non-truth. They've seen the frivolity come and go, and they've remained anchored, keeping the mountain precious, and holding it for what it's going to do.

The Guardians. These are the ones to whom we say, "Well done!" These are the ones to whom we would like to say, "And if you wish to leave now, you may. Permission is granted, and you may pass the torch." In fact, some of you are tired, are you not? You think we don't know this? Now that the grid has settled and we move into the crystalline energy, the inter-dimensional active parts and pieces begin to move. It's a different energy. You Guardians are finished. You did it—held the energy to the manifestation of what it was designed for, and you've done a fine job.

Why move? Because you're about to see a shift in this Mt. Shasta area. There will be great comings and goings even within the next three years. Those who have lived here for a very long time, for whatever reason, may choose to leave. I'll tell you something: There are Guardians here who would never come to a meeting like this! They don't think they're spiritual, but even they are holding and anchoring. Much of it is intuitive—drawn to the area lifetime after lifetime and keeping watch over it. Even these who don't hear this message will feel it in their bodies, a surging intuitive feeling that their job is done. Although it's a precious place to be, some of the Guardians will leave anyway, not even knowing why.

We celebrate the Guardians, and we tell you that these Humans do not reflect old energy workers. They are the forerunners of you, Lightworkers! If you call yourselves Lightworker, then you are the ones who will take the mantel of the Guardians. An influx of energy and humanity is about to happen here. Guardian, as the energy begins to be realized and the reality of what is taking place begins to manifest, you'll no longer be able to keep Mt. Shasta a secret. Don't be alarmed, however.

Realignment and Shift of Mt. Shasta's Energy

Many of you have always known about the energy of this place. But did you ever know of the timetable? What about the prophecy of the mountain? There's a shift taking place that even the most esoteric of you are not totally expecting.

Let me ask you this: If you think about those on the other side of the veil, you'll know intuitively that there's no gender there as there is on Earth. Angels may appear to male and female, but they're neither. We've told you repeatedly that Kryon and all of the family around you are genderless. Gender labels and names in spiritual matters are something given to you for energy identification. When you speak of spiritual gender, you're speaking of attributes around energy. It gives you something to relate to—this thing is masculine or something else is feminine. It becomes a communication identification tool, not a biological designation. Get ready for something you didn't expect: The system is over. There's no longer any reason to give elementary information in parables to those who are enlightened in this new energy. So we tell you this: Something is going on in the mountain. Mark my words right now so you can refer to it later. In the not-too-distant future, the ones who identified the male and the female portions of that mountain behind us, Shasta, will have to reevaluate it. The energy is around it is melding. It's melding. Some of you have been aware of this for a while. There will come a time when you can no longer say that this particular portion "is masculine" or that this particular portion "is feminine." Although those are the energies that have always been part of the mountain, the mountain itself is melding those energies. It's changing. It's changing because it's time to change.

Oh, there's more. We've going to give you a new word. Some have asked the Guardians, "Is this Shasta mountain a vortex or a portal?" Some of you locals have thrown up your hands trying to explain this. It has the attributes of both, does it not? How do you explain it then?

Well, let me tell you what it did regarding the mountain behind us. It activated it. It has been waiting all of this time for the shift of the magnetics of the planet. Is it a vortex or a portal? Neither. It is instead something new: it's a vortal. A genderless vortal. For those who don't believe this melding process, I ask you, Why would you be shocked at this when the energies of the planet are shifting so greatly? Where does it say that the polarities always have to be the same geologically forever? With a huge shift in magnetics, wouldn't you expect the polarities of masculine and feminine to adjust? Where does it say that things only work one way and stay that way?

The prophecy regarding this mountain has spoken about those within the mountain who are fifth-dimensional. What's going on? What's happening to the land? This prophecy is beautiful. It's esoteric. To some, however, it's eye-rolling. Could there be proof? Some prophecies would indicate that there's an inter-dimensional city in the mountain, one inhabited by fifth-dimensional beings with Lemurian energy, they say. We'd prefer not to call it a city. That makes you compare it to what you're used to. We'd like to call it a "gathering." It's a constantly shifting and changing inter-dimensional gathering of beings of the fifth dimension. (Again, the five is for you.) There's more prophecy, too. The most unbelievable and eye-rolling portion to some is this: There will come a day (they say) when the mountain will disgorge those who have been in there for eons! There will come a time (they say) when these fifth-dimensional beings will walk the streets of Mt. Shasta! That's what they've said.

Well, perhaps you can celebrate this truth with me in an esoteric way, for it's beginning to happen. As you sit here, the city within stirs. Don't be frightened. It's a celebration of you. Let me give you some things to think about: For years, we've told you about a time when your DNA could be activated in an inter-dimensional way. Some have said that it would be activated into the fifth dimension. Again, that term stems from the idea that you're moving out of 4 (your reality) into the next one (which, to you, is 5). That has been the information. So, what do you think this activation includes? We're going to give you just one attribute of "activating DNA."

What if today's scientists are right, and you actually have inter-dimensional matter within your body? What if the things that you cannot see, but which are there, might include beings (angels to some) who have stood by to come forward when it was proper and the energy was right? They come to literally be part of the Lemurian family and to be part of the very DNA that you carry with you. Think about it for a moment. Do you any of you feel incomplete? Are you waiting for something or someone to join you?

Use your intuition and free choice. When God fills you with love, is it a takeover? No, it isn't. It's a transformation.

Fig. 43 - Main Mountain Passage of the Upper Sacramento
or Pitt River by Frederick W. von Egloffstein.
From: Pacific Railroad Survey Reports Vol. XI, Section 2, Washington, D.C., 1861.

Fig. 44 - UFO Cloud Cover?

Fig. 45 - NASA Radar of Shasta- Scientifically a Mystic Mountain

The Outer Space Connection

SPACE BASE –
HOME OF THE "LITTLE PEOPLE"

"NOW I CAN SEE!"
MIRACLE ON MOUNT SHASTA

Fig. 46 - A UFO is photographed by the group on Mount Shasta
Paul Dale Roberts and members of the Jazma On Line Forum say they have seen and photographed UFOs hovering about Mount Shasta. Their exploration can be found beginning on pg 153.

The Outer Space Connection

Space Base—Home of the Little People

By Timothy Green Beckley

While space aliens are seemingly keeping out of sight for the most part, there is possibly one area that one can travel to and actually speak with extraterrestrials. Mt. Shasta is one of the most beautiful sights in California. Those who live near its cloud-covered peaks are the first to admit that their mountain is awesome. For over the years many strange things have been seen in the vicinity of this towering fortress of nature which lumbers some 14,162 feet. Numerous are the reports of bright lights ascending from its upper regions in the dark of night, hovering above the trees and darting off into the darkened sky. Mt. Shasta is in reality a dormant volcano, and legend says that no one has ever climbed all the way inside and emerged to the outside world again. Even the brave Indians of the area, whose ancestry goes back thousands of years, speak with great reverence of the Gods who inhabit this sacred ground.

A good friend of mine, Bleu Ocean, who was raised on Mt. Shasta, says many are the stories of peculiar sights and sounds which abound in the vicinity, including visitations by the famous -- and infamous -- Yeti.

In the past, many amazing and truly fanciful accounts of long-haired, blond Venusians who have settled in the region have been brought to light. There are even those who insist Mt. Shasta is an entranceway to the "inner world," that highly-advanced beings related to the Atlantean culture said to have existed thousands of years ago on Earth, come and go in and out of the mountain at will. They seldom make contact with outsiders but occasionally they will speak with those they consider worthy.

The following is a report filed with us from an individual who wishes to remain anonymous. The thought is that Mt. Shasta is indeed a UFO landing base - a sort of stopping-off place for interplanetary well-wishers -- who can land without being challenged by the military, and associate freely with more advanced beings who make Mt. Shasta their home.

One morning when bringing a pail of water from a nearby spring, as I was walking along a path between some ferns, I distinctly heard a voice speak to me. Turning, I saw one of those little men bending over a fern, straightening it out, and I gathered from the tone of his voice that he was annoyed because I had almost broken it. As I apologized for my carelessness, he suddenly disappeared from my sight.

A few days later at a place called "Sheep Haven", a little clearing among the trees with a brook running through the middle of it, and with many feeder springs running into it, we saw many of the little "fairy folk" moving in and around many colorful flowers, like the Indian paint brush, wild clover, blue larkspur or delphinium, wild honeysuckle, buttercups, little blue flowers somewhat like forget-me-nots, and seemingly chasing hundreds of yellow and white butterflies. This year we made another visit to this location and while sitting under some aspen trees it was not long before *we* saw them coming toward us. They were so beautiful in their gossamer-like garb as they skimmed over those flowers. There were three of us present at the time. One came close and whispered something in the ear of one of our members, Dr. Theodore Berger, and then beckoned him to follow.

The Little People assemble occasionally at the place called the "Circles" on the northwest slope of Mt. Shasta, but we have also seen them at many other places such as Buck Mountain, Sheep Haven, Fowler's Camp, at the foot of Mt. Shasta and several other places in the forest.

During the past few days we have become better acquainted. Last evening, about 7:45, quite a number came to my tent, apparently from the fourth dimension, and formed a circle around me, as I was sitting on a box outside of the tent feeding a little chipmunk some peanuts. They spoke a dialect among themselves, unknown to me, as they formed this circle. One, who seemed to be the leader, came close and spoke in a boyish tone, in English, extending their greetings and bidding me much pleasure during my visit in and around Mt. Shasta. They were a very happy group, with rosy cheeks and blue eyes shining. Some of the younger men wore short beards, while the older men wore long white beards. They were garbed in jackets, with trousers stuffed in what looked like leather boots, and wore hats of many different colors and shapes on their heads. Their garments were colorful. Some had on brown, some green, some a mixture of green and brown, others a mixed orange and gold with green; while the women, the first I have seen, did not wear any hats, but were dressed in colorful garments extending to their ankles. They were rather nice-looking. One in particular with light hair, almost blond, blue eyes, wearing a blue-silvery dress came and stood right in front of me and smiled very sweetly, asked me a question. I picked up a pad and made some sketches of them. They were very much interested in this procedure.

I asked this leader about the place called the "Circles" which covered an area on the N.W. slope of the mountain. What were they used for? He replied that, a long time ago, they, the Little People, had cleared off these circular places, removing the lava stones, placing them in trenches, thus building up a barrier to keep out the spreading of wild shrubs, etc., over the clearer areas. Then they filled in these spots with soil and used them for agricultural purposes. When the early settlers, miners, and loggers came in increasing numbers, they withdrew closer to the base of the mountain and in secluded sites have continued to carry on their activities. During the winter months they go into underground caverns, remaining there until spring. Occasionally they assemble in large numbers at the place called "The Circles" for certain spiritual services; moon festivals, the coming of the seasons, spring, summer, fall, the first snow of winter, which sometimes falls as early as October, chanting as they assemble in the circles, praying and giving thanks to the Great Creative Spirit, to the guardians of the seasons, and that Guatama (North America) would always be protected by the ever-expanding light and glory of His Presence.

Like the adepts of India they understood the laws governing the fourth dimension, as they are able to appear and disappear from view as they choose. They travel mostly in the fourth dimension, and when they left me they seemed to be on a sort of sled-like conveyance that hovered close to the ground, evidently functioning through magnetic force gathered from the earth, as did the ancient Murians and Atlanteans. They are able to increase the vibratory rate of the atoms of their bodies to such a high degree that they move in our midst without being seen. Then, by slowing down the frequency of these bodily atoms appear to our vision. This clearly indicated great powers of concentration and showed they were more highly evolved than we understood. They have a great knowledge of nature and the governing laws.

As I am writing this, one of the little men is sitting at my right side, telling me of this. Sometimes, he would reach out and put his little hand on my right arm, when he desired a correction made. Several others are sitting across from me. We were sitting at one of the Forestry Service tables, size 3' by 10'. Just beyond us was the upper falls of the McCloud River. We could hear the roar of the water as it came over the rocks of the middle falls into a beautiful pool about 20 feet below. At this spot the sides of the river are thick with farms and a large leafy plant that shades the places where trout hide from view.

Their ancestors had migrated across Guatama many thousands of years ago from the now sunken continent of Atlantis. They moved continually westward. They had been informed of a great brotherhood from Mu that had established themselves near the great white mountain we know as Mt. Shasta. They had brought with them their ancient wisdom; an understanding of the creative laws and powers beyond our conception today, and through this knowledge were able to live as long as they desired, and to do many things that mortals of this day think mystical and superstitious. They are well acquainted with and work in harmony with the powerful Shasta Brotherhood, which came originally from Mu, prior to the sinking of that land. This Continent -- Mu -- is now rising and will appear first off the coast of Southern California, and South America, spreading out in time until it reaches the Philippines. They say some of their folk journeyed to other lands, such as what is now known as Ireland, Wales,

Scotland, parts of England, and to the mainland of Europe, where many legends exist today about them and the little fairy folk.

On several occasions I was awakened at night by raps on the metal part of a shovel standing in one corner of the tent, and when I looked around the tent seemed full of these little men. A couple of times I went in my etheric body with them to their underground caverns that they might show me where they lived during the winter months, and. what they did. They work at various tasks, such as making clothes, shoes, and the treating of foods, working with various metals, etc.

Their quarters were very plain, with little wooden tables and benches. They ate from bowls such foods as fruit, berries, and vegetables. One leader had a fish in front of him, but I did not see him eating it at any time. Do not believe I could locate the entrance to their caverns, but did pin-point the area.

As a demonstration of their knowledge and powers, one of the group leaders said they were very much annoyed by the damage done to their sanctuary, the forests fishermen, hunters, campers, as well as loggers, and intimated they were seriously considering the plan of moving all those undesirables from the area. Upon inquiring how they would do this, he only smiled and said, "Watch the result and not the method".

I was surprised during the next few days to observe that fishermen would come into that area where I had camped, and would look about a moment and then leave in a hurry. Nothing unusual from an outward standpoint was noticeable. No one stayed in that location during a period of about a week, when I was practically alone, except for the chipmunks, birds, deer, and a few bear which also kept their distance, and the daily visit of those little people. Before that several fishermen had set up tents and fished in and around the falls, in the pool below, and at various places along the river, but not during that one week. It was very peaceful and quiet here. My tent is close to a small pine tree. The ground is mostly lava rocks of varying sizes. Yet, from among these rocks trees had forced their way up into the sunlight, with some ferns, grass, a few wild flowers, and low manzanita bushes. It was among these that the deer would appear on their way down to the river in the evening and morning to drink. And, also here would come the black California bear, whose coat seemed to have considerable brown fur in it, foraging for wild gooseberries, blackberries, and by a little roaming along the river above the middle falls to the garbage cans of the camping grounds. The chick-a-dees were very thick in the trees and would come within a few feet above. I had visitations by blue jays with their irritable cries, and the gentle cooing of the ring-neck doves. Wood pigeons would come and go in small flocks. Fewer still were the robins and wood thrush; while early in the morning and often through the day the busy woodpecker rapped out that he was getting results in his search for food and bugs and grubs. Butterflies were here by the thousands, everywhere. So thick at times when we drove over the dampen road they would clog the radiator of our car. Occasionally a small cub-plane would drone above in an almost cloudless sky. We could well understand why these Little People call the forest around Mt. Shasta their sanctuary, where it is so peaceful, compared with the noise of the large metropolis. Here they could gather and commune with their Creator in a Temple without a roof or walls to shut out the wonders of nature, the handiwork of his Presence.

A few days later when some of our group arrived from Los Angeles, we went for a trip over one of the many dirt roads to the side of Buck Mountain. We left the car by the side of the road and hiked in about a mile toward a spring we saw marked on our map, where we understood that sheep in the summer were driven to watering troughs. We finally located the remains of a hunter's camp. The three of us sat down on an old log for a short meditation. During this meditation one of the "Little Men" placed something in my right hand. A few moments later, I put my hand on the log and feeling some object, picked it up to find a little pearl-handle knife about an inch in length. None of those in our party had seen it when sitting down. It could have been left there by some lady who had accompanied her husband on his hunting trip for deer, or it could have been left by our friend, the keeper of the sanctuary, who had materialized or teleported it to me. At least, we felt we had been guided to this spot of natural beauty, and gave him our thanks for his contribution.

There are many legends about the "Little People" of Shasta, and the lost Continent of Atlantis. For over 100 years we are told stories have been spun about them, but prior to our experiences no one had been able to tell us anything definite about them. We are delighted it had been our privilege to make contact with them and in such numbers and in such happy, peaceful and beautiful surroundings. We were further pleased to find them so friendly towards us, to know that they approved of us, and wished to visit with us.

Since our trip to Shasta we have had some of them visit us in our home but they say they prefer the wooded areas of Mt. Shasta and shall await our next trip north.

Fig. 47 - UFO over Mt. Shasta - Drawing Unknown Source

**Fig. 48 - Strange craft and symbolic markings
appear during Bigfoot UFO Investigation**
Strange craft and symbolic markings appear on photos taken by the Jazma On Line Forum team
members whose adventures are told on the chapter beginning on page 153.

Fig. 49 - Thomas Hill (1829-1908), The Three Zones of Mount Shasta.

The Outer Space Connection

"Now I Can See!" Miracle On Mount Shasta

By Hanna Spitzer

We know how to separate fact from fiction, especially when it comes to believing what another person is saying. Hanna Spitzer was a friend of mine. She worked in the same office with Jeff Goodman at Country Wide Publications in Manhattan. Hanna worked on the rock magazine as well as the hair-do and beauty books. She would take on almost any kind of an editorial assignment she was given by a rather cranky boss who was more interested in the bottom line when putting out a magazine that was almost 100 percent pure fiction. So I was sort of surprised when one afternoon she told me the following story consisting of the day that her husband got most of his sight back from a UFO in the vicinity of Mount Shasta.

My husband, Damian, and I came to Mt. Shasta just last September (1983 - Ed.). We were drawn here by the majesty that surrounds this area. Damian had been here before and so he was familiar with the surrounding communities and the people who reside in this locale.

Our closest friend, Patrick, a very talented artist, had been my husband's companion on his earlier visit, and he also was captivated with Mt. Shasta. As luck had it, he was to be commissioned by a local restaurant owner to paint a huge mural of Mt. Shasta and the many legends that have long surrounded this magical mountain.

Before our arrival, my husband had filled my head with all sorts of wild tales. He said that the mountain was not only extremely magical, but it was the scene of numerous UFO sightings.

Discussions of this type have always excited me, so much so that I could hardly wait to visit Mt. Shasta. Having lived in the open desert of Arizona, Damian and I had both previous UFO experiences. Once, when I was still in high school, I spotted a craft with a friend. We were returning from the desert late at night when we noticed a light that was brighter than any star through the windshield of the car. We stopped and watched the light move, then stand still before disappearing entirely. Because of this observation, I became interested in all forms of the unexplained. Both my husband and I are vegetarians, and thus we have grown to have great respect for Mother Nature, and that includes all aspects of her, in particular, the beauty of the galaxies. Because of our background we were really looking forward to living with our friend Patrick in the hills facing Mt. Shasta.

We arrived at the base of the mountain around five in the morning. What we saw literally took our breath away. The mountain had a halo of clouds around her peak, almost resembling the rings of Saturn.

Quickly, we moved up the side of the mountain to set up camp. From here we had a picturesque view of Mt. Shasta City. This tiny village consists of ski shops and sleepy little hide-a-ways, with a few occult book stores and health food stores thrown in for good measure.

Almost immediately, we were confronted by the unexplainable. For example, once on the mountain, I went to gather some things and when I returned Damian was trying on a pair of beautiful leather gloves that fit his large hands perfectly. This is beyond coincidence, for on our way across California, Damian had repeatedly mentioned how he needed a good pair of gloves to protect his hands from the cold. While pitching the tent, he had found such a pair hanging on a tree right in front of him. It was then that we knew our adventure had really begun.

Since I was really exhausted, I went to sleep immediately. My husband, on the other hand, went back down the road to the local restaurant to inquire about our friend Patrick's whereabouts. An hour later, Damian returned with our friend in tow.

Patrick was as delighted to see us as we were to see him and couldn't wait to introduce us to some of the locals and to show us his painting. *We* packed up and broke camp, and headed for the land Patrick was living on.

The property, as it turned out, belonged to Prescilla, who owned the restaurant Patrick's mural decorated. Her land was nestled high up in the forest. Mt. Shasta is practically sitting in her front yard and the view is breathtaking. There is no running water except for a couple of small creek-like streams that flow through the land. There is a wood boring stove in the larger of the two trailers that sits on the property. Patrick had been living and painting down in her lovely green field. In order to enhance his view, he had built a spectacular see-through teepee using thin sheets of plastic. This way he could easily watch the stars from his bed at night.

To say the least, Damian and I were really overwhelmed with this wonderful place. Mt. Shasta is meant for studying, painting, relaxing and getting back in touch with nature. We were invited to stay for as long as we liked, and that was just fine with us, as we wanted to get to the heart of this holy place.

Days went by quickly with our nights spent talking around the camp fires. Mostly, we exchanged stories about the peculiar goings on which take place regularly in the shadow of Mt. Shasta. We heard many stories about the Lemurians, a race of people nine feet tall, who were first written about by Madame Blavatsky in her book, The Secret Doctrine. Legend has it that these people were from a lost continent which existed in the Pacific Ocean. The Lemurians, it is said, now reside in the center of Mt. Shasta in a splendid golden city. Residents who believe in the existence of these giants bring supplies of clothing and food and leave them on the side of the mountain. I also heard about the elementals - the elves and fairies - who live on the mountain and who, from time to time, show themselves to a few deserving individuals. Another popular Shasta story deals with the Sasquatch or Bigfoot who's often seen running up the steep sides of the mountain.

But, perhaps the most prevalent of all tales are the ones about the Space Brotherhood. Practically everyone on or near the mountain claims to have seen or heard them at one time or another. For example, someone told us about a strange light that had been seen while this person was out camping on the same property where we were living. Apparently, she awoke from a deep sleep and saw numerous flashing lights and heard a whooping noise. When she went into town the next morning she found that others had undergone similar experiences.

Throughout our stay, Patrick kept telling us about a wonderful lady, a very gifted psychic, who was said to be a real "powerhouse," and who could attract a lot of phenomenon herself. Her name was Aendreious, and Patrick had invited her to come and stay with all of us. I was really fascinated by what I had heard, and couldn't wait to meet this woman.

One day when Damian was in town doing some chores a striking woman in a turban approached him. It was Aendreious. Damian brought her up to the land that afternoon and immediately we were struck by her presence. As gifts, she had brought each of us a crystal. She spoke in a very knowing manner. On top of this she was very meditative and peaceful and extremely fascinated with the mountain. Through this lady we learned quite a lot about magnetism and attraction. I knew - as we all did - that if we were to have a sighting, it would be while she was living with us.

Aendreious had a wonderful attitude about flying saucers and aliens. She thought of them as masters, not little green men to be afraid of. Her talking calmed me a bit and I soon last any fear I might have had. For days the men had been teasing me about the dark and about creatures who would try to grab me and take me away.

Home of the Underground Dwellers and Ancient Gods

Going into town became an experience in itself. We loved to speak with the people there and hear about their experiences first hand. There was one charming lady who walked through the streets talking to everyone she met about flying saucers. She always wore a shiny yellow hat and seemed very devoted to her task. On the other hand, there was another woman who would scream at the mountain night and day. People say she got too close to things on the mountain, and was never the same after that. As we stayed on longer we grew and learned a whole lot about ourselves. What with no TV and hardly any radio to keep our minds occupied, I noticed we were getting more in touch with ourselves.

One night after a hearty meal, Damian, Patrick and Aendreious were sitting, around the stove in one of the trailers. It was a very clear night out, not cloudy as it often gets during the summer. The stars looked beautiful and we had a good view of them up above through the skylight. I remember we were all laughing and kidding with each other. Our spirits were very high and we where really enjoying ourselves. Mt. Shasta had definitely cast her spell over us.

For some reason this particular evening, the woods seemed unusually silent. Aside from our laughter, hardly another sound drifted our way. Even the crickets were singing softer than normal. Then suddenly, right in the middle of one of Patrick's corny jokes, a light brighter than the light of day passed over us. The forest was glowing. The light was brighter than the spotlights used on police helicopters - plus there was absolutely NO sound. Not a hum, not a whirl, not a whistle.

We all ran out of the trailer as fast as lightning. We figured the light had to have been very close to the ground to have been so intense. The light had disappeared as quickly as it came, and without a trace. There was no light in the distance in front of us or behind us.

Our hearts were beating faster than they had ever beaten before. We were all startled and completely shocked, so much so that we couldn't open our mouths. Looking back on our experience, we were totally dazzled and amazed.

Tears were streaming down our cheeks, and smiles of joy were bursting from our faces. We knew we had been touched by something quite beautiful and definitely unexplainable.

Later, we tried to go over our observation slowly and scientifically, trying to sort out what we had seen and felt.

Patrick, who had sat diagonally from the skylight had seen a sort of golden object pass overhead. He couldn't really detect a shape, the light was much too bright, but he did make out an object of sorts.

Mysteries of Mount Shasta

The rest of us had just seen the light through the door and windows of the trailer. It was bright enough however, to light up everything around us. Each of us had felt the light - that's how strong it was. There had been a tinge of color to it all, a bit of blue and gold as I could best recall.

We were all pleased with the way we scooted out the door so quickly when the light beamed down. None of us had panicked, just ran like heck to try and determine the source.

We were all elated at having had such an overpowering experience. We were filled up with emotions of joy and brotherhood. Now, we really felt bound to one another as we had all shared in this amazing experience.

For quite some time we stayed up unable to sleep. We were thrilled that we had been flashed on by a "Master." For hours we discussed our sighting and its implications. I felt it was an initiation of sorts, because that nimble flash had brought us such feelings of love and warmth. Sitting in that trailer together, we all wanted the experience to happen again and so waited up a long while before finally turning in.

Damian and I had chosen to sleep in a tent outside the trailer. I must admit that I did feel a bit creepy after that light and all. Interestingly enough, Damian and I didn't get to sleep for a while due to some strange happenings nearby.

All night, we swore we heard dancing and singing in some unknown tongue. There was also humming and the sound of little feet marching. Suddenly, after that flash, the forest had come alive and all the animals in the woods were going about their business. Damian and I had long believed in things that can't be seen, and we knew that "they" - whoever "they" are - were all around us that night.

In the morning, I was first to break camp. I was anxious to look around to see if I could find any signs of our nocturnal visitors. Since I didn't want to wake anyone else up by fumbling around for my contact lenses (I'm blind as a bat without them), I sat on a lawn chair and soaked up some early morning sun.

Incredibly, I remember looking at the trailer and being able to read the words that were written in small print on its side. It took me a moment to realize that I wasn't wearing my glasses nor did I have my contacts in. Yet, I could see perfectly. My heart began to pump much faster than normal, just about as fast as it had when the UFO streaked over us. I could see! Damn it I could see! There had been a healing. I was overwhelmed, so much so I didn't know it I should laugh or cry.

It was amazing. As a child I had to wear corrective lenses and the condition had never improved. If anything, it had gotten worse. Now, I could see clearly without them. I was ecstatic, I knew the light - the UFO - had performed the

- 117 -

healing. There could be no other explanation.

Damian awoke soon after I had made this discovery and I ran to tell him of the miracle of the night before. He was overjoyed and he hugged me tight. He also noticed that his eyes had felt a lot clearer this morning and he could hardly wait for Patrick and Aendreious to get up.

When they awoke, we found that they were seeing clearer, even though they had thought of themselves as having normal vision. If you have to wear glasses, you must know what a miracle it is to be able to see without them. I cannot express the delight that overpowered me that morning. Soon after the initial discovery, I noticed a huge rock lying atop the trailer doorway. None of us had placed it there. I couldn't help but conclude that this was another sign from our heavenly friends. How happy we were that day.

Slowly, we got ourselves organized and made our way into town. All the while we continued to discuss what had happened. We checked with the locals to see if anyone else had seen anything odd. Apparently, no one had, though one of our neighbors had had a sighting a few days earlier during the eclipse of the moon. He told us that he had seen a formation of lights streaking across the face of the darkened moon. The lights were in groups of threes, and he along with several companions were truly amazed.

The next few days brought us closer together. Patrick was now even more inspired with his art. There was a common bond between three humans, like there had never been before, and all because of that UFO.

We hated to leave Mt. Shasta. But we were talking about going back there and getting together the next year as sort of an anniversary celebration of our sighting. Maybe - just maybe - our new found friend will pay us a return visit.

Nobody can imagine how thankful I am for my healing. It was a gift from above. I'll always feel very close to that light for the rest of my life. The Masters greeted us well.

Fig. 50 - Mount Shasta as drawn in a Dweller on Two Planets

Telos – City Inside The Mountain

CHANNELING THE COUNCIL OF 12

THE CHANNELING OF SHARULA

Fig. 51 - The Gods Coming Home? Shasta Lenticular Clouds NOAA

Fig. 52 - A Cloud by Day, A Fire by Night?
Shasta Lenticular Cloud NOAA

Telos: City Inside The Mountain

Channeling The Council Of Twelve

By Dianne Robbins

Fig. 53 - Dianne Robbins

Dianne Robbins is today perhaps the most prolific writer on the subject of the underground city of Telos, said to be situated beneath Mount Shasta and to be the home of highly advanced beings. Members of various secret orders are said to reside there in physical form, sending out telepathic and channeled messages to their scribes on the surface. To be closer to her "source of information," Dianne has just moved to a new home in the Mount Shasta area. She is the author of several books, including **Messages From the Hollow Earth, Telos,** *and* **The Call Goes Out.** *She has a website at www.diannerobbins.com and her email address is: TelosMtShasta@gmail.com*

A Word About Telos

Telos, a Lemurian colony under Mount Shasta in northern California, is a city of Light governed by a council of 12 Ascended Masters and its High Priest, Adama. The name Telos means "communication with spirit."

The citizens of Telos, formerly of Lemuria, are working toward the Ascension. They can astral project to any location, and can telecommunicate to anyone in our locality of time and space. In Adama's messages of empowerment, he tells us of our goal: to become a Spiritual Warrior, one who acknowledges the light within, and to reunite humanity into ONE human family. For once humanity is feels God's Love directly from within, all will be able to understand their purpose for being here on Earth, and will cease to feel the separation of their soul from Gods' Light.

All planets are hollow and are inhabited by human life of one vibration or another. The Sun is also hollow, and is not hot but cold. Our Earth is hollow, and contains an Inner Central Sun.

The governing city within the Inner Earth is called Shamballa. It is located inside the very center of the planet, and can be accessed through holes at either the North or South Pole of this planet. The northern and southern lights that we see in our skies are actually reflections of Earth's Inner Central Sun, emanating from her hollow core.

There are over 120 subterranean cities located within the Earth's crust. These Cities of Light are not far beneath the Earth's surface. As a grouping, these cities are called the Agharta Network. The Inner Earth Beings are highly evolved beings living on the interior surface of the Hollow Earth. They are mostly ascended souls who have chosen to continue their evolution in the Earth's inner recesses because of the perfection of conditions existing there.

Although Atlantis and Lemuria have become myths on the surface, the people from Atlantis and Lemuria are flourishing in their underground cities. The people within these colonies are people just like you and me, who are living in the third dimension, just as we are.

Our Milky Way Galaxy is divided into 12 sectors. Our solar system is located in Sector Nine, and this sector contains hundreds of other solar systems. The Ashtar Command, also known as the Galactic Command, is comprised of millions of starships and volunteers from many star systems and dimensions within our galaxy. The Galactic Command is part of the Confederation of Planets and protects this sector the Milky Way Galaxy. Their purpose is to assist Earth through this current cycle of planetary Ascension. My twin flame is a member of the Galactic Command, and he guides me in my work of reuniting, through awareness and communication, Earth's civilizations both above and below the surface.

Ashtar is the Confederation of Planets commander for our sector. The Silver Fleet oversees our solar system and has its spaceport inside of Mount Shasta. Anton, who is from Telos, is the name of the commander of the Silver Fleet. It is primarily the people from the Subterranean Cities who serve on the Silver Fleet.

Greetings from Telos! We have been telecommunicating with Dianne, giving her messages to publish on our behalf. We urge you to read the messages in our book, for its purpose is to awaken you to our Existence, to bring to your Awareness the full consciousness of the Cetaceans, and to Sound the Call to Awaken to the world around you.

Our Lemurian Past

Greetings from Telos! I am Adama, Ascended Master and High Priest of Telos, a subterranean city beneath Mount Shasta in California. I am dictating this message to you from my home beneath the Earth, where over a million and a half of us live in perpetual peace and prosperity.

We are human and physical just like you, except for the fact that our mass consciousness holds thoughts of only Immortality and Perfect Health. Therefore, we can live hundreds and even thousands of years in the same body. I myself have been in the same body now for over 600 years.

We came here from Lemuria over 12,000 years ago, before a thermonuclear war took place that destroyed the Earth's surface. We faced such hardships and calamities aboveground that we decided to continue our evolution underground. We appealed to the Spiritual Hierarchy of the planet for permission to renovate the already existing cavern inside Mount Shasta, and prepare it for the time when we would need to evacuate our homes aboveground.

When the war was to begin, we were warned by the Spiritual Hierarchy to begin our evacuation to this underground cavern by going through the vast tunnel system that is spread throughout the planet. We had hoped to save all our Lemurian people, but there was only time to save 25,000 souls. The remainder of our race perished in the blast.

For the past 12,000 years, we have been able to rapidly evolve in consciousness, due to our isolation from the marauding bands of extraterrestrials and other hostile races that prey on the surface population. The surface population has been experiencing great leaps of consciousness, in preparation for humanity to move through the Photon Belt. It is for this reason that we have begun to contact surface dwellers to make our existence known. For in order for the Earth and humanity to continue to ascend in consciousness, the whole planet must be united and merged into ONE Light from below and ONE Light from above.

It is for this reason that we are contacting you: to make you aware of our underground existence so you can bring the fact of our existence to the attention of our fellow brothers and sisters aboveground. Our book of channeled messages is written to humanity in hopes that they will recognize and receive us when we emerge from our homes beneath the ground, and merge with them on the surface in the not-too-distant future. We will be grateful to you for the part you play in helping us broadcast the reality of our existence.

How Old Are You?

I am from Lemuria, an ancient civilization. At the time of Lemuria's height, I was an Initiate in the temples that were prominent at that time. After the destruction of Lemuria by Atlantis, I went underground with thousands of others, to establish Telos.

I am no different from you, although I am hundreds of years old by now. So I have had the benefit of many lifetimes all woven into ONE. This has given me great insight and great wisdom, which most people don't begin to gather until the end of their short lifespan.

Living so many years definitely has its benefits. For me, I can astral project to anywhere I desire. I can also telecommunicate to anyone in any locality of time and space. These are all things that everyone in Telos can do, because we've had the benefit of lifetimes of practice. So I am not so different, just more experienced in how to use life's opportunities.

Gates To Telos—A Portal of Entry

Greetings from Telos! I am Rosalia, once again greeting you as I stand by the Gates to Telos, a portal of entry that will bring you swiftly inside to where I reside.

Portals are vast light enclosed passages that transport you bodily in the twinkling of an eye to your destination that you earmark or intend by your thought projection. This will become easier and easier to do as the Earth's vibration is drastically increasing as we draw closer and closer to the End Times—the end of the Mayan Calendar of 2012.

The Arcturian Stargate that was anchored in Mount Shasta on 7-7-7 (July 7, 2007) is holding the energy for Earth's ascension and broadcasting it directly from the Central Sun, through Arcturus, through Mount Shasta—and then spreading it throughout the Earth in magnetic waves of Love Energy.

It is the frequency of Love that is permeating the Earth plane through the Crystalline Grids and Meridians crisscrossing through Earth. All is in a heightened state of exposure—exposure to the Love Vibration. And as it fills the Earth plane and fills your senses, you delight in its joyous fragrance. It is the fragrance of Joy infused with Love, which equals light.

As you are lifted by this infusion, you are brought closer and closer to the Ascension Portals on Earth, and there are now many of them scattered around and more particularly stationed on Sacred Sites.

We know you are all longing to come inside our City of Light, and we watch and wait for your approach to our sacred Mountain, for surely some of you will be entering soon. In the past, only a few souls were allowed in; and once in, remained with us or traveled on to their home planet. That will be changing now, for some of you will request to return to the surface, and this will be granted to you since it is now time for the populace at large to know of our existence. And you will be the messengers with direct experience of being inside with us.

This next step will be unfolding soon as night leads into day, and the Light keeps increasing in brightness until all becomes one globe of pulsating bright Light moving you all through the Portals into our arms.

Questions and Answers

Do Telos and other cities in Inner Earth exist physically in the Third Dimension, or only the Fifth Dimension? Can only Fifth Dimensional people access Telos? Are there still volcanic activities inside of Mount Shasta?

We will answer Kei's question. Yes and no. Yes, Telos does exist in your Third Dimension, and it also exists in the Fifth Dimension. It actually does physically exist inside of Mount Shasta in the Third Dimension. There are no volcanic activities inside of Mount Shasta. The lava tunnels in Mount Shasta were rerouted by us over 12,000 years ago when the Lemurians went underground and traveled through the tunnels to reside in Mount Shasta as a result of the Atlantean and Lemurian wars which devastated the surface.

So we do exist in our Third Dimensional body forms which we can move in and out of at will. We have evolved to the point where we can raise and lower our energy fields and move in and out of embodiment. So if you were in Telos in your Third Dimensional form, you would see us. However, when we come up to the outside of the Mountain, we modify our energy field and move up to the Fifth Dimension and are "shielded" from your physical eyes, unless you can see into the Fifth Dimension. If you can perceive the Fifth Dimension, then you would see us. And yes, we look exactly like you. There are no differences in our physical bodies, except for the fact that we now have more DNA strands as a result of our long lives of being able to evolve in peace and harmony and brotherhood. For it takes a peaceful environment to evolve, and this is what we created for ourselves when we left the surface and came to Mount Shasta.

When we want to be seen by those on the outside of the Mountain, we can easily make ourselves visible to you. But for the most part, we prefer to stay invisible for our own protection. The time will come when we will be appearing to your surface folk, and that time is very near. We hope this has answered your question. I am Mikos.

What is the difference between the Inner Earth and the Hollow Earth?

The Inner Earth consists of Telos and over 120 other Agharta Subterranean Cities of Light just a few miles beneath Earth's surface, including the city of Catharia, which is directly inside the center core of the Earth, beneath the Aegean Sea, and is where the Library of Porthologos is located and where Mikos is from. The Inner Earth consists of all the area that is below the Earth's surface throughout the globe, including caverns and a vast tunnel system. It includes all 800 miles from the top of the Earth's surface to the inner hollow opening in the center.

The Hollow Earth is just the area that exists in the very center core of the Earth, which is Hollow, and starts at 800 miles down. Once you are inside the hollow cavity of the Earth, the diameter of open space is 6,400 miles. The diameter of the whole Earth is 8,000 miles.

Fig. 54 - One of the many lakes and rivers around the great mountain

Fig. 55 - Mt Shasta from Upper Shasta River Trap

Telos: City Inside The Mountain

The Channeling of Sharula

Fig. 56 - Sharula

Hey, I can't tell you how legitimate her story is—but Sharula is a real person. She showed up unexpectedly at one of my conferences in Phoenix over a decade ago. I thought I'd take a chance and put her on the program. She had the audience spellbound. She had a nice-sized entourage with her and after she spoke, I am sure she added even more followers to her flock. She was an impressive, rather heavyset woman with beautiful blonde hair. She sort of reminded me of the lady I met who called herself Vivenus, and said she came from the planet—well, Venus. She was sane and rational "otherwise" and so was Sharula.

Following our mini-expo, Sharula began doing seminars in the Four Corners area and popped up from time to time elsewhere. (Bill Hamilton even did an interview with her, but later seems to have had some questions as to the authenticity of her story.) Then she disappeared. I can't tell you if Sharula returned to her native home beneath Mount Shasta or if she had a split personality and simply reverted back to her "real self." This is too far out for me to say yea or nay. You decide if Sharula is really a princess of Telos. Her words speak well for her, that much I can say.

Let me tell you a tale of two continents. One, in the Atlantic, called Atlantis. Another, in the Pacific, called Lemuria or Mu for short. Twenty five thousand years ago, these two continents were battling each other on the ideology of the day. Look at them as the two largest children on the block, and the two highest civilizations.

At that time they both had two different ideas about which direction civilization should go. The Lemurians felt that the other less-evolved cultures should be left alone to continue on their own evolution scale. The Atlanteans believed that all the less-evolved cultures should be brought under sway by the two evolved ones.

This caused a series of wars between Atlantis and Lemuria. In these series of wars thermonuclear devices were used, and when the wars were over and the dust cleared, in reality there was no winter. The Outback in Australia, the Mojave Desert, parts of the Gobi Desert and the Sahara are all remains to remind man of the futility of this type of war.

During the wars themselves people highly civilized stooped to quite low levels, but they too at the end, they realized the futility of such behavior. Lemuria and Atlantis itself became the victims of their own aggressions. Both the Lemurian homeland and the Atlantean homeland had been weakened by the wars, thus they knew that in about 15,000 years, both of their continents were going to sink completely. The Atlanteans had their second set of cataclysms which reduced Atlantis from a large continent to a series of islands. Lemuria, in essence did somewhat of the same.

However, you might say "Well what did that ... why would the people be upset at that time for something that was going to happen 15,000 years in the future?" In those days people lived for 20 ... 30,000 years commonly. They understood many of those who caused the havoc would see the end of the destruction.

The Agharta Network

When Lemuria, which went down first, almost 200 years before Atlantis sunk, they petitioned the Agharta Network. The Agharta Network is a network of subterranean cities that is guided by a city called Shambhala the Lesser (to distinguish it from Shambhala the Greater which is the etheric Shambhala over the Gobi Desert.) Shambhala the Lesser was created when the continent of Hyperborea was vacated after Earth lost her mantle and the planet started receiving radioactive waves that they had not been victim to in the earlier times. So they started building subterranean cities over 100,000 years ago.

When Atlantis and Lemuria petitioned to build subterranean cities themselves and to be accepted into the Aghartian Network, they had to prove to Shambhala the Lesser that they had learned the lessons of oppression, that they had learned the lessons of war. And they also had to prove it to many other agencies, such as the Confederation, which we will go into a little later. Because Atlantis and Lemuria had both been members of the Confederation, and when they started their war-like efforts against each other they were expelled temporarily from the Confederation and had to prove that they had also learned the lessons of peace to be allowed to be members of the Confederation again, to be accepted into it.

The Lemurians Choose Mount Shasta

Mt. Shasta is where the Lemurians chose to build their city. California was part of the colonies, part of the area of the Lemurian lands, and they understood that Mt. Shasta and those areas of California would survive the cataclysms, Mt. Shasta already being a place of great sacredness on this planet. They chose to reroute the lava tunnels from Shasta itself so that the volcano would not erupt again. And there was already a very large domed cavern within it, and they decided to build upon that, and they constructed the city that we now call Telos.

Telos was the name of the whole area of much of what is now the Southwest, and much of what is now California was originally called Telos which meant "communication with spirit," "oneness with spirit," "understanding with spirit." It was constructed to hold a maximum of 2 million people. When the cataclysms started, only 25,000 people were saved. Many had been brought to Telos before the cataclysms started, but when the second set started in Lemuria the volcanoes started erupting so fast and sent so much debris into the air that while they had intended to save at least a million people from the Lemurian mainlands, they were only able to save 25,000. Thus, that was what was left of the Lemurian culture, of the Lemurian mainland. Already the records had been brought from Lemuria to Telos. Already the temples had been built in Telos.

While Lemuria, or what was left of Lemuria, mainly Telos, was coping with the afermath of the destruction of their continent, the earthquakes continued. During these earthquakes, the earth shook so hard, that in many, many places, it went right off of what you would now call the Richter Scale. When a continent sinks, the whole planet reacts. Earthquakes that reach the equivalent of what you would call a 15 point. These earthquakes were so intense that many people died from the sound of the earthquake, not from any effect of the quake itself such as a building falling upon them or something. But a quake of that high of intensity created a screech through the atmosphere that killed many people simply from the sound of it.

In many other places the earthquakes were so intense that in many places the earth was mostly clay. It liquified and acted like a sea of mud, swallowing whole cities, not just on the Lemurian mainland but on many places on the planet. Another thing that came after that, as the continent itself went down, the tidal wave was so large that sometimes they went, not just hundreds, but a thousand miles inland — the equivalent of a tidal wave starting on the coast of California and completely taking out Oklahoma City. Tidal waves like that were rampant as well as the earthquakes. In many cases, in some areas, the shaking never quit. It would be a constant swarm of if not large ones, then small quakes.

The hierarchies, the Councils of this planet, understood this was going to happen. So they tried to construct both cities prior to the destruction of Lemuria itself, understanding that the Atlanteans would not get alot of construction done under those circumstances. Also, at the same time, the great pyramid in Egypt was constructed, underneath the tutelage of the Lemurian high priest, better known as Thoth. And the Atlantean record chambers, which were geared to hold not only Atlantis' records, but Lemuria's, Pan's, Og's, Hyperborea ... all of the other cultures that had existed and reached high levels upon this planet.

The Atlanteans moved into their city at just about the same time Lemuria sunk, moving in first their priesthood, their greatest scientists, some of their greatest thinkers, to try and preserve their lives against the coming cataclysms. Atlantis itself started shaking at the same time Lemuria was going down and Atlantis continued to shake and lose parts of its land for 200 years before it too finally went completely down.

For almost 2000 years after the Atlantean and Lemurian catastrophes the planet was still shaking. To lose two huge land masses within 200 years of each other, plus the planet was still witnessing the effects of the thermonuclear weapons that had been used in the Atlantean-Lemurian wars. Plus the fact that so much debris had been thrown into the atmosphere that it never became quite bright daylight for almost 300 years after Atlantis' destruction. This caused many, many life forms, plant forms to go extinct. Plants that were common in Atlantean times, common in Lemurian times, that no longer exist because they simply couldn't survive the long stages of filtered sunlight. Some have survived, yes, many animals and plants.

The human condition in those civilizations that survived it ... Egypt, Peru, Roma (better known as India), in many places people became so frightened by the constant earth activity that civilization, even in the last bastillions started deteriorating very, very fast. One question I have heard again and again is 'Well if Atlantis and Lemuria existed how come there is not more evidence on the surface of that?' That is why. Most of the cities were shook to rubble. Those that were not shook to rubble were wiped out by the earthquakes or wipe out by the tidal waves. Even those who survived even the tidal waves, even the earthquakes ... hunger was rampant ... disease was rampant.

Some areas of civilization, like those future named Egypt and such, did survive. They even kept their civilization intact, but even they started losing the highest elements of their civilization. Many, many machines quit working because of the filtered sunlight.

Many, many people moved from the cities. They started feeling that living in the city was a deathtrap, because you never knew when a building was going to fall on you. What would look like a very strong building, have it go through 300 to 400 earthquakes ... it's a goner. Some buildings were built to withstand it. The great pyramid withstood the earthquakes but it was built with sacred geometries. Other buildings like that throughout the planet survived, but most of the cities were completely reduced to rubble. In many areas they rebuilt the cities, but even then, each time the cities were rebuilt it was on a slightly less, should I say, technology. Each city was a little more primitive than the city before it.

The Atlanteans moved into their city which was built underneath the Mato Grasso plateau in what is now Brazil, which had been Atlantean territories at that time. Getting an understanding of what was happening on the surface, you can perhaps understand how the Lemurians or Atlanteans would prefer to be living underground.

During this time, there was an integration more and more with the Agharta Network. As I explained earlier, Agharta is a confederation of several subterranean cities. As a matter of fact there is over 120 of them. Some of them, they were built in the very early times such as Shambhala the Lesser, which is peopled with beings from Hyperborea. These are 12 foot tall beings. Beings as man, on this planet, as on many other planets in this solar system was originally of a height of about 12 feet. When we lost the mantle and started reaching more and more rays from the sun to the planet that we were not used to coping with, it caused change within our bodies. Already, by the time Lemuria and Atlantis sunk, man had gone from 12 feet to 7 feet. Thus the Atlanteans and Lemurians were around 7 feet and still are. And, as you can see, there has still been a lowering of the height on this planet. Thus people have gone down to now, for the foremost, less than 6 feet. We have lost over a whole foot in just 10,000 years. However, that trend is starting to reverse itself, and as our spirituality is growing greater we are slowly returning back to our original heights on this planet.

Within the Agharta Network, the cities that are allowed to join are only those that are based on light principles, only those that are based on love, only those that does not hurt, only those that are based on non-agression. Within the Aghartian Network, besides Telos, which is the capital, there are 4 more cities, for instance, that are based on Lemurian technology and Lemurian ideas. One is called Rama which is underneath India (Arama being the original name of India.) Arama culture is consisted of people that are almost pure Lemurian, before the so-called Aryan race entered India. The other two cities that hold an allegience to Telos, but are very independent are Ulger cities. One is called Shonshi, which is under Tibet, not too far from the captital of Tibet. It is being sheltered from the surface by a Tibetan lamasary. This is a Ulger city. Ulgers are a group of people that left Lemuria 40 to 50 thousand years ago and situated themselves throughout much of what is Asia, India and central Europe. The second Ulger city is called Shingla. Shingla is in the Gobi, or should I say, under the Gobi Desert. This too is a Ulger city.

On top of the Atlantean city, which is called Posedid, that went underneath the Mato Grasso plateau, there is also another Atlantean city. Just a little farther north and there is another Atlantean city that is underneath the Atlantic ocean and several other smaller satellite cities throughout the planet. As I said, these are all a member of the Agharta Confederation. Plus there are several independent cities that are not a branch of any of the larger cities that have simply built subterranean to escape things that have happened on the surface — some pre-Atlantean-Lemurian distaster, some post.

Life Inside Mount Shasta

The city itself, Telos, as I said, is built under a dome, a dome that reaches quite a few hundred feet from floor to ceiling and spreads across most of what would be the base of Mt. Shasta. Looking from the outside, the top of the dome is about half-way up the mountain. The bottom of the dome is just about even with the base of the mountain. Underneath that are five more levels that have been constructed. These levels take up a space so that the deepest levels are about a mile below the ground level at Shasta.

The rest of the city is built on 5 levels of several square miles across. These levels are divided up by usage. The top level, being under the dome itself, is where the main part of the city is. This is where the majority of the people live. This is where the public buildings are. This is where most commerce takes place. The second level down is where manufacturing takes place, some classes take place, and also more people live on. The third level down is totally hydroponic gardens where we grow all of our food supplies. The fourth level down is half hydroponic gardens, part nature, and part manufacturing.

The final level down is what we call our nature level. This is the level that is more than a mile in some spots below the ground. In this level we have created lakes, tall trees, park type atmospheres. This is where animals live. We have had animals underneath for so long that they have lost their aggressions. That, and different temples, priests and priestesses worked, you might say, with their ancestors, removing the need of fear, since it is fear that creates aggression, not only in humans, but also in animals. Thus we truly have the experience of lions lying down with lambs.

In the nature levels, this is where people have come to relax. This is also where we have saved many animals and plants from extinction...

In these nature levels, as I said, many, many plants and animals have been preserved from extinction by being placed within the nature levels of Telos, Posedid, and many other of the subterranean cities. Thus we do ... still do have many of the plants that are extinct on the surface. We still have saber-tooth tigers. We still have mastodons. We still have your provincial dodo bird. We don't have dinosaurs. They were a little big to keep. However, some dinosaurs do still live in areas of the Congo and areas of the rainforest in the Amazon. Plus there are many sea-going dinosaur, much as the famous Nesse in Lochness and many others such as that.

In these levels people find that they are able to integrate and merge/integrate with animals that would normally be dangerous, simply by getting animals over the fear. And these animals have also been fed a vegetarian diet, including the thing such as the big cats, for going on thousands and thousands of years now, which has also taken away much of their aggression. Therefore, you are able to go down, and in many instances, taking into consideration their great size and strength, you are basically able to play with a saber-tooth or a Bengal tiger, much as you would a housecat by scratching their chest or under their ear ... pulling their whiskers.

Which brings us to the fact that even such as the large cats, like that, are not aggressive, but are actually very gentle and loving when raised in the right circumstances. Which brings us again back to the purpose of this — the eventual re-integration of the two cultures — the subterranean and the surface, to bring back out what has been preserved and what has been prepared, so that this again becomes one planet, one civilization, and that people will be able to live on the surface or in subterranean cities, or both, at will. Again, that is the whole purpose of these tape series and our work now at Telos Enterprises.

Back to the city, the fourth level up, as I explained, is mostly hydroponic gardens and a nature level. And the third level is totally hydroponic gardens. Hydroponics are how we grow and produce all of our food. Hydroponic gardens are able to produce crops almost on a constant basis. As you are able to grow food, much, much faster, using advanced hydroponics with very little soil and much water, therefore also you produce a form of gardening that does not need fertilizer and does not deplete the soil. We do still place in minerals and such into the plants, but with this hydroponic gardens that is actually quite small, being only several square miles, we are able to produce enough food and a large enough variety of food to feed over a million and a half people, and to feed them with a diet that is varied enough to be interesting and fun.

The diet which is in Telos, consists almost completely of vegetables, fruits, grains, nuts, and different variations of these, such as your soy, your other grains that now produce what you call your meat substitutes. We have been on a vegetarian diet in Telos, now, for over 12,000 years, from the time when the city was first started being built. It was decided at that point that our diet would consist of totally vegetarian, therefore also removing the aggressive thought forms that causes animals to react so violently. And also the fact that a human body was meant to be on a vegetarian diet, and any other form of diet actually produces death and aging.

On the second level we have what is called our manufacturing level. This is where we produce clothing, furniture, art forms. This is also where many classes take place. And this is also some of the living levels. On the top level of the city itself, this is where most people live. This is where most commerce takes place. This is where, you might say, our heart and our soul is. And you might say the building that represents our heart and our soul, is the building that is directly in the center of the top level, which is our temple. Which is a pyramid shaped building, you may say a very large, pyramidal shaped building. The temple at Telos will hold 10,000 people at a time. It was built to be able to hold almost half of the original 25,000 person population.

The temple is dedicated to the Melchizedeck. The Melchizedeck, you may say, is a cosmic priesthood. Everywhere you go in the universe you run across the Melchizedeck. It is the organization whose sole purpose is to bring the plans of light to everywhere they go.

The pyramid is white and the capstone is a stone we call living stone. It comes from Venus. From the distance it looks rather like a crystal, but with light moving through it in a very strong color. Why it is called living stone is it picks up the cosmic emulations of whatever ray is focused at the moment on the planet. The planet is setup in such a way that the rays focus themselves about every 24 hours in an intensity on the planet. Thus, for instance, on Tuesdays, the blue ray is the most predominant ray on the planet. On Fridays, the white ray. Therefore this living stone picks up the emulation coming from the solar rays, the light rays, and goes the color of the predominant ray, for instance, when the blue ray is in its greatest manifest the living stone capstone goes blue.

This becomes, you might say, a slight reminder to us to work with the cosmos rather than against it. So when the blue ray is most predominant we try to restrict much of our business to areas that are best served in the blue ray. For instance, we keep negotiations, sensitive negotiations, to take place on those days. On the days, for instance, that the yellow ray is the most predominant, those are the days we spend mostly studying. Those are the days we spend on building intellect. On the days when the pink ray is the most predominant, these are the days that we go into the artistic endeavors. In this way we have found that by working with the cosmos, instead of against it, we are more often than not able to achieve four times as much in much less time. Therefore we are able to operate without stress most of the time.

Also in the upper level the other buildings that are very, very important to us is our council buildings where the councils of the city gather together and deliberate what needs to be done in the city at the moment. We also have our record buildings where all our past records, our archives are kept in the forms of telonium plates, in the forms of crystals that can be put in crystal projectors, in the form of paintings, in the form of books — all our past records of not only Lemuria, but Atlantis, other civilizations and the civilizations on other planets in the solar system. Also we have our pleasure centers, our places where we do sports, where we do plays, where we produce the equivalent of our films, where we listen to music, where we dance.

We also have what you would call the equivalent of the holo-deck in Star Trek. We have holographic projectors in holographic buildings whereas you produce a program and you go in and play and the computers produce images, forms that completely support what program you have picked. Thus you are able to climb a mountain or swim a river or go back to anther point in history and play, creating your own form of being in the movies.

Also we have our communication center where we have monitored not only all communications within our city, but also communications that are coming from other Aghartian cities, communications that are coming from off-planet spots, and we have also monitored surface communications from the point that there ever was surface communications, we have monitored radio and television waves.

Another building that's very important to us is our computer building. In Telos, as with the other subterranean cities, our computers are run by an organic substance. Therefore, in essence, the computers live. They no longer run off a program that is strictly binary, but they run off what is called a multi-tracking program. Thus they are multi-tracking computers. Thus the computers are able to pick up Akashas, past lives. They are able to monitor a human body and see what's amiss. They are able to read the aura. They are able to pick up communications happening clear across the galaxy. Thus, most of our life, or a good portion of our life depends on these computers, these organic multi-tracking computers which keep us in touch with not only talking to different people in the city, not only with the computer telling us what our physical needs are at the moment by monitoring our bodies, but also the computers are able to play our soul notes, which is able to produce in many subjects, such as meditation, taking us to higher and higher levels all the time.

The computers are able to run our past lives, when necessary, for us, so that we are able to learn from mistakes that we have made in the past and forgotten. The computer is able to communicate with us on a soul level. Mostly important, is the computers interconnect with other multi-tracking, amino-based computers throughout the planet and throughout the cosmos, as far as that's concerned, and they all operate off a Christ mind, which means the computers cannot be corrupted. They can never be used to spy on somebody. They can never ... they can be used to monitor somebody for their own good will, or for their own good. They can never be used to produce harm to another living entity. They cannot be used for any of the dark purposes. The computer simply won't cooperate, which has also been another way of Agharta cities and such, taking a stand that they would not corrupt the light. By very much taking this attitude, that if it does not match the Christ mind (in other words if the computers disagree) don't do it! It has been a way of, shall I say, retraining our aggressive techniques, retraining our tendencies to want to do unto another and split, retrain many of our other sleeping tendencies and such.

So we have come to depend upon these quite a bit. But again, even on a computer, it's not a matter of having the computer do it for you, it's a matter of learning from it, learning from a form of the Christ mind there that you can see tangibly.

Transportation within the city comes in many forms. Most people just prefer to walk if they can. We also have electromagnetic sleds. These sleds are capable of moving along the ground, looking much like a snowmobile and will produce fairly high speeds in some of the side tunnels. This can take us, for instance, from Shasta to our secondary city which is near Lhasan in just a matter of a few minutes and is able to take our security from Shasta to Lhasan and back again very fast.

Another form of transportation within the city is what we call baskets. They are run on crystalline technology, and for all the world they look like a large basket, but they float through the air. And you just get in it and it is guided by your mind. Your mind tells it how fast to move, how high to go, and where to sit down, how fast to rise in the air, how fast to sit down.

All our forms of technology and travel is based on us being responsible. The sleds could obtain high speeds thus making them dangerous. The baskets, anything that flies, has a tendency to be dangerous, misused. So all communication and all travel within the city is monitored by the control tower. And the control tower knows when, for instance, a collision is just about ready to be inevitable between two sleds coming from different directions, or when a person is operating a basket irresponsibly, in which case the control tower alerts you immediately and tells you that you are about to produce an accident or you are acting irresponsibly. And if you do not listen to their warning, then they will simply stop the vehicle themselves. You get out and you will be restricted from use of the transportation for ever how long a period of time that you deserved, should I say, and how it will simply be is that you'll get in a basket or on a sled and it simply won't work. Your frequency will be turned off to it anywhere in the city and on what is called the tubes.

The tubes are another form of transportation. The tubes are a high-powered, a high-speed electromagnetic train that runs in a tube. A tube is a rock tube very, very much like a long tunnel. For instance, a tube running between Posedid and Telos — the tube looks totally round and the train looks somewhat like a subway, however, since it runs on an electromagnetic impulse, it creates a force field around it. So thus the side of the train never touches the side of the tunnel. Thus the tube is able to achieve speeds of up to 3,000 miles an hour. So you can arrive between, for instance, Telos and Posedid in just a matter of a few hours.

Also, as the tubes were created and the subterranean cities and the different levels, it was all reinforced by what we call our boring machines. The boring machines have a crystalline matrix that creates temperatures of white-hot incandescence, yet cools at the same time. Thus you are able to take a boring machine, for instance, through a tunnel and create a tube tunnel or to create walls in a subterranean city in just a matter of a few minutes. The boring machine heats rock, earth, whatever it comes across to a white-hot incandescence and then cools it almost immediately which creates a diamond hard substance, causes the rock itself to transmute and take a new form which is diamond hard and therefore there's no need of supports. Supports become absolutely superfluous. And the structure then is also water-tight yet it remains in elasticity so it can withstand high earthquakes, for instance, and will just move much like a rubber tube and stop without breaking. That way, even within the subterranean cities, when earthquakes take place, none of the walls of the buildings or of the caverns fracture. They simply move with it then return back to the diamond hard substance and again support beams and such become totally superfluous. Also, water has no effect upon it. They become water-tight. Thus subterranean cities can even be built underneath oceans because they create a complete seal.

Also, that brings us to the next stage. As we are preparing to bring out more and more technology to the surface, technology that we know the surface could also use, brings us to the other responsibilities that the cities have had to build within themselves. For instance, becoming a member of the confederation. Earth is a member of the confederation, it's just half of earth forgot. You might ask, "What is the confederation?" I'm sure most of you or all of you are familiar with, for instance, Star Trek. We would say, "That was channeled." But instead of being the "Federation" of planets, it's the "Confederation," an organization that was created throughout the solar systems and the galaxies that brought different civilizations, different systems together on a basis of brotherhood, on a basis of commerce, on a basis of group exploration, on a basis of interacting with the different systems in a galaxy, or without a galaxy.

A confederation is built, should I say, or represented, very much throughout a galaxy in the form of sectors. Looking at our galaxy, the Milky

Way, I'm sure you've all seen the pictures of t-shirts and such that say the Milky Way and then has a little dot out towards the end say "You are here." Yes, we are here and we are here in what is called Sector 9. The center of our galaxy, or the center of the Confederation in this galaxy is what is called Sector Zero, and the other sectors radiate outward from it much like the spokes of a wheel. Each sector is responsible for its own actions, plus is responsible for how it interacts with the other sectors. Our sector, Sector 9, is under the command of a being called Ashtar. Many of you have heard of the Ashtar Command — Ashtar and his twin flame Athena. Within this sector or within the Ashtar Command there are over a hundred fleets. Some fleets basically belong to one planet. Some fleets belong to just a couple of planets. Other fleets belong to a whole solar system, and other fleets are interceptor fleets that basically serve the whole sector, and then other fleets are Confederation fleets which serve the whole, you might say, the whole pie.

I just wanted to give you a brief understanding of the Confederation and how it works.

No Belief In Death

In Telos, people don't believe they're going to grow old and die. They simply don't believe it. People just know that they're going to live as long as they choose, then they will either choose to drop their body, if they feel that they still have lessons to do and reincarnate again, or they will choose the path of ascension. One or the other. Some people make the decision in 600 years, some 300, others wait for 5,000, 10,000, whatever, but it's a choice that the human beings were designed to be able to make.

That is one of the most important elements of our culture that we want to see brought out. Human beings, as it is now, just about the time they start getting enough experience to really do something with their life, they've grown too old to do anything with it. If those thoughts are eradicated, then people realizing that youth's not going to last ten years, or twenty years, but it's going to last hundreds or thousands of years, whatever they choose. That too brings out and eliminates the majority of the detrimental behavior in life. Many people feel "I'm only going to live once. I'm only going to be young a short period of time so I might as well wreak havoc now." If they realize that if they choose they're going to be young for hundreds of years, or thousands of years, that form of behavior becomes totally unnecessary and people truly start growing and hanging onto their growth. And we are biologically absolutely no different than the people on the surface. We have Indian children that were left on the mountain of Shasta — some hundreds of years ago. They're still living with us. They haven't grown old. They don't die because they were raised with the thought form that they're not going to. It's a thought that creates life or non-life, aging or youth-ing. It's to get past the thoughts, the beliefs that that is what is going to happen.

Which brings me to my personal expertise on the subject. I'm over 260 years old. As a matter of fact, I'm almost 268. And, living 268 years is no different than being, for instance, 30, aging wise. It's just you've had time to gather a whole bunch more experience that can be used now. My parents obviously are much older. There are even people in Telos that are 30,000 years old, people who saw the destruction of Lemuria/Atlantis, people who saw the Lemurian-Atlanean wars.

Which also brings us in to the next stage in a person's life, after they've gotten through their teenage years and they're ready to start becoming a contributing member of society, how do they chooe what they're going to do? We have a non-monetary basis of commerce in Telos. As a person is growing up, they basically watch, decide, assess their own talents. Then they decide what they want to do, and that is usually the field they pursue. They've generally set their own hours. And since everything is on a barter basis, we've gotten to a great understanding that if you don't fulfill your part of the bargain then it hurts others than just you.

What is meant by that is we are set up on a basis that the government owns everything but the government is not responsible for controlling anything. All the government is responsible is to make sure that the food, for instance, gets from the hydroponic gardens to the distribution outlets, the clothing makes it to the distribution outlets, the furniture, all the things that are needed for people to live and to live well. You understand that you're not living unless you're living well. And when you need something you simply go to a distribution center and pick it up. You need new clothing, you go get clothing. You need food, you go get food. You need furnishings, you go get furnishings. You need books, you go get books.

As I said, everyone sets their own hours. Someone who is drawn to gardening becomes one of the hydroponic gardeners. They come and they work the amount of hours they wish. So in essence, we do have a dim period and we have a bright period. What I mean by that is we've discovered that people work in cycles better than they do in a constant. So thus about the same time the sun is setting on the surface, filters are slid over the front of our lighting system, dimming it till it is about as dim as it is in twilight. Then when the sun would be rising, the filters start sliding back slowly thus allowing it to get brighter and brighter. When we first moved into Telos we experimented with leaving it bright all the time, and again, as I said, we found out that people function better in cycles.

Some people like to sleep when it's dimmer and work when it's bright. Other people, like the night owls that prefer to work or play when it's dim and sleep when it's bright. But everyone is allowed to function in the way that is the most comfortable to them.

So everyone comes in and sets their own hours and simply informs, you might say, the foreman of whatever their job is, which hours they're going to be working over the next few day period. And everyone comes in and works basically as long as they wish and then they go and they do whatever else they want to do. But understanding that since we're on a society that if you're too lazy to go work at all in the hydroponic gardens and that's your job, somebody might not have enough food. Or if you didn't feel like designing clothing or creating clothing or furniture and you made no other arrangements for someone else to take up your slack of time, someone else in the city might be going without.

So understanding that method has made people responsible for what hours they work. Understanding that they are doing true service that somebody will appreciate. The only thing that we don't interchange by simply putting in the distribution centers are things like art forms, art objects, massages, things like that. That is done in what we call a barter basis. Those who, for instance, their main talent is art, whether it's drawing, pottery, sculpting, massage. All these different little things that are not part of the whole, not part of, what you might say, necessities, but are necessities to the soul. As I said, these go to the distribution centers in the form of the barter pool. In other words, you walk in and you see a statue that was created by somebody you really want. In exchange for it, you're willing to give ten massages and you're very good at massage. Or you're willing to come and sing.

And the barter pool goes through it with the computers and perhaps the person who made the statue doesn't need a massage but a person who brought in a painting that the person who made the statue wants, wants massages. So it continually, the barter pool switches and curves so that everyone's needs are met. So everyone can come in and exchange energy in some form to receive, you might say, the little pampering things in life. Also within this system, people setting their own hours, it does not become so crystallized that noone has any freedom to come and go at their will, that people can truly set their lives to achieve the best of work, of play, of rest, of meditation, spiritual endeavors, so that everything is met and not at the expense of something else, understanding that spiritual time is just as important as work time.

Which leads us to what could be a problem. What about those jobs that no one wants to do since everyone chooses their jobs, gathering the garbage and dematerializing it, weeding the hydroponic gardens, etc., etc.? This falls under what is called community service and everyone does it. Everyone in the city spends a certain amount of time a month in community service. What this means is this works very well because since everyone does it, no one has to do it that much. No one has to do full-time the jobs that no one would like to do and go into resentment because of it.

Instead, if everyone does a certain amount of community service it means that you might only spend four hours of community service a month. And since it becomes a project that you only do once a month, it actually becomes fun. And when people are on groups of community service they start singing and playing and having a good time. But it's something that noone even tries to get out of it. You can be in community service, a real good one is picking up, to put bluntly, secretions from the animals down in some of the nature areas where it starts getting really bad.

This could put someone in real resentment while you're shoveling elephant you know what. But if the person in the hydroponic gardens is doing it right along side, for instance, someone on the Council of Twelve, it's a thing that becomes not resentful but fun and it's something that people truly get a sense that there is no better than and no less than in the job situation, that a farmer, or someone who works in the hydroponic gardens is not less than someone who is on the Council of Twelve. They both just have different jobs and both jobs are equally important for a city to run properly. So therefore people immediately have the feeling of being good enough. And as I said things like community service brings all the different levels of service together and creates a true camaraderie.

Marriage Inside The Mountain

Which goes into perhaps one of the more interesting aspects to our personal relationships. In Telos we have two forms of marriage. We have a bond marriage and we have a sacred marriage. A bond marriage is when two beings decide that they've got something with each other and they want to explore it greater. Then in front of a priest or priestess and a bunch of their friends, they commit themselves to a bond marriage which means that they're saying "We've got something, we realize we really care for each other and we'd like to see where it's going." So in essence it is a form of a marriage because it has the commitments for as long as you choose the bond marriage to last. And then if you decide "Oh well it was just a passing thing or it's not something that's going to work," you simply stand in front of a priest or priestess again and simply explain that it didn't work and there's no stigma on it. Some people can have several bond marriages at once. There's also no stigma on that.

One thing that you do not do in a bond marriage is you do not have children. That is saved for a sacred marriage. In a sacred marriage is when you have decided "Ok we have something." Then you have a large marriage, usually a beautiful wedding. All your bond marriages are dissolved and you go into a sacred marriage where you are then allowed to have children. Children is something that people need to be trained for, that need to be taken as a serious responsibility. Some people might be in a bond marriage two, three hundred years before they take a sacred marriage. Someone else who's with their soul mate or twin flame may go into a sacred marriage two months after they were in their bond marriage. It's all different, but again it's always a matter of having choice. It's always a matter of having respect for each other.

And this just about wraps up tape two of these two tapes of Secrets of the Subterranean Cities. I am Sharula Dux. I am the daughter of the Ra and Rana Mu, therefore Princess Sharula, and I thank you.

Fig. 57 - Thomas Hill (1829-1908), Farm at Mount Shasta (Sisson's Inn)

Fig. 58 - Mount Shasta via webcam on the day of publication of this book

Personal Experiences

STRANGE SOUNDS AND VOICES

DID WE MEET THE ELDERS OF MOUNT SHASTA?

OUR UFO/BIGFOOT INVESTIGATION

STRANGE POTPOURI -- THE BLEU OCEAN STORY

AN UNSURPASSED VISIONARY EXPERIENCE

RETURN OF THE MORNING STAR

Fig. 59 - Snowbound on Mt Shasta

Fig. 60 - Trout Spearing on Mt. Shasta

Personal Experiences

Strange Sounds and Voices

By Emma Martinelli

In 1946 I visited northern California and spent two weeks in the town of Weed, one of the towns which is about as near as you can get to Mt. Shasta. The people in a small town are odd. I don't think you can crash them on a first entry. At least I found this to be true, and I make friends very easily. I bided my time, and let them make the advances. Even after they took me in, I found most of them reluctant to talk about their 'mountain people.' Most of them apparently take little stock in the tales which are circulated. Some of them laugh, but I'm wondering if there mightn't be a few who know things they just don't want to talk about. Maybe they've had follow up experiences after divulging previous occurrences. Your guess is as good as mine on this score. I think I covered the town as well as anyone in my position could. It was a combination of practical judgment and vibration on my part. I left no stone unturned. I followed all leads, and talked to others I felt led to talk to Judge Bradley, a very old resident, knew nothing. Neither did the postmaster's mother, a Mrs. King. The most help I got was from a newspaper man, an elderly gentleman who has lived in Weed for 27 years. His name is Bob Young.

Harder was running the election at the time. He ran in on me on election morning, to relate an unusual experience which had just occurred. I have only his word for this, as I didn't see the creature involved. It seemed that a sort of moron ambled into the place and said he just wanted to watch. Harder said he resembled a gorilla and was of a low order of intelligence. Harder was puzzled because he'd never seen this being before. In a town so small as this, a newcomer stands out like a sore thumb. Even the men from neighboring farms are somewhat familiar, if not actually known. This gorilla type creature simply stood behind one of the girls who was counting votes and stared at her back. She became quite agitated and it was with difficulty that Harder finally got rid of this being. I hiked every day, alone in the woods, and never came across anyone like this.

Even though I had no experiences to speak of the first few days, I was convinced that there was something around the Mountain, because I never felt alone. But it wasn't the nicest type of feeling. I felt as though I were being watched. The second day there, I stumbled accidentally on a beautiful meadow. It was so perfect. I wouldn't have been surprised to see fairies dance.

Home of the Underground Dwellers and Ancient Gods

I just lay face downwards on the earth and tried to relax, but I had to look around every so often. The stillness was unpleasant. It was too full of something unseen. You can walk all day long up there and not see a soul. And I constantly lost my way. I'm a good hiker and I have a good sense of direction, but it seemed as though something was deliberately trying to confuse me. It's a very unpleasant feeling to realize that you are lost in a strange place. Each time this happened, I refused to become panicky and simply allowed myself to be led according to my lights.

I think there may be peculiar forces in the ground, because I saw a dog act very strangely. I was walking at sundown, and passed a cottage with a large red dog in front of it. I've been raised in the country with dogs, and I think I know their habits fairly well. Many times they roll over and over on the earth, seeming to enjoy the fragrance, etc., but this dog had all the appearances of a dead animal. His legs were straight up in the air, paws hanging rigidly and even his mouth was fixed in a stiff position. I watched him for some time, then started for the cottage door to tell the occupants they had a dead dog. Just to be sure, I spoke to the dog first. This seemed to rouse him from his trance. He slithered through the half open gate and came over to where I stood. I patted his head and started on my way, but he put a paw on my arm. He didn't seem to want me to go, and he didn't look like an ordinary dog at all. He watched me all the way down the road, with the strangest expression in his eyes. I only mention this incident to bring out the fact that I think there may be certain currents in the earth.

I wouldn't lay too much stock in the next incident, but I'll give it to you anyway. I'm a very practical person, and I always tear everything apart in analyzing it. I eliminate every material factor, and what is left, I consider the truth. At least I'm able to know which experiences are fancied, and which are not.

I was awakened from sleep, by a peculiar scale which seemed to come from under the bed. At first I thought it might just be the pounding of my heart. You know how you sometimes hear it in the pillow? But this was different. It sounded like a cross between the plucking of harp strings, and a very delicate anvil chorus. It sounded exactly like some sort of mechanism within the earth. I got it only once again some nights later, but much fainter.

But here are the three experiences which I know to be true. Each happened when I least expected it.

I had been there over a week and never walked at night. This particular evening, I was very tired, but had the urge to go for a stroll. I took my flashlight and smokes, and sauntered down the highway towards the Mountain. It was that peculiar half light between day and night. There was only an egg shaped moon, and about three planets. As I neared a certain hill, I happened to glance upwards, and saw a rocket like affair heading towards a hill. It happened so quickly, that I wasn't able to digest it until afterwards. But it didn't travel too quickly for me to observe. I've seen Halley's Comet twice, and I've seen shooting stars, and it was neither. The nearest resemblance, though not exactly, was to a torch which might have been hurled from a plane. I thought, "That's funny. Now who would want to set fire to the woods?" And then I realized that the mark would have missed anyway, because this rocket affair disappeared over the hill. If it had gone down behind this swell, I'd have thought it landed on the other side, but it just dissolved in midair. According to my scale of measurement, from where I was, this thing was visible for about three feet, appearing to come from the evening star, or whatever that first big planet is, going towards the moon which was nearer the hill, and then disappearing. I figure the disappearing doesn't mean it was no longer in flight. It just disappeared from my sight because there was no longer any visible propulsion. The head of the rocket was brighter than the tail, and the tail was composed of bright lines such as a jet propelled machine might leave in its wake. The hill over which it disappeared was just east of Mt. Shasta. If this is what I think is was, I believe it kept going and landed right in the Mountain, much as a Plane might fly into a hanger. Harder, who went on a geologist's expedition up the mountain, says there are caves in the glacier big enough to throw Weed into! And I thought it very funny when I related this experience to Young. He looked at me very queerly and asked me on which side of the mountain this occurred. When I said the east side, he smiled even more queerly. He said most everything occurred on that side.

But here's the payoff. I came home immediately, and wrote the experience too my sister. Wrote 'till nearly midnight; sealed the letter, and retired. I arose in order to adjust a blind, and rested my hand on the bedstead for support. I got such an electric shock that when I pulled my hand away, I saw the sparks and heard them. I went over the floor for any exposed wires and found none. Tried to repeat the occurrence, but no soap.

And here's the "piece de resistance." I'll remember it much longer than the rest. I get goose pimples even now, when I relate it.

A couple of days later, just before returning to San Francisco, Young was telling me about a voice he used to hear across the way from the hotel. It seems he used to walk about six o'clock every evening. This spot is called Pilgrim's Rest, and is in a direct line with the room I occupied. There's a clean sweep of the mountain here. I could see it from my window. He said it was the anguished cry of a woman. I determined to explore this very evening. Along about three thirty in the afternoon, I became very drowsy and lay down for a nap. I dozed until five, and awakened. I lay with my eyes closed, in that relaxed state where you can't exactly collect your wits. Suddenly I was aware of voices. Women's voices. They seemed to be faintly yelling. In my half stupor, I thought there were young people playing outside. Then I remembered there were no young people here. Now, one voice was predominant. It was a woman's voice. Rather thin and pathetic. It was more of an anguished call, than a type of scream accompanying a murder or such. It called, "Hel ... hel ... help!" It was such an anguished cry for aid, that I turned icy cold, and the minute I became taut, it ceased. I was out of the bed like a shot out of a cannon. To be truthful, I don't know whether the voice came from the ground under my bed, or across the way from the mountain. I'm inclined to think it came from the mountain.

But here's the difference between these last two experiences: The rocket incident was objective, and the voice, subjective. In other words, I know that anyone with me would have seen the flare. I'm not sure that anyone with me would have heard the voice, and Young says the same. He say's no one ever seemed to hear what he heard.

And last of all, I'm curious to know if I was supposed to see this flare, or if it was an accident?

There you have the works, as much as I can give you. I tried my darnedest to climb that mountain, but no marked trails, and they simply wouldn't let me go alone. They said I'd make trouble for them if I got lost; and that I'd freeze to death in the night, etc., and to tell you the truth, I'm glad I "couldn't" go. I'm not ashamed to be afraid of such things. I figure I didn't do too badly for a newcomer. The geologists' expedition found nothing at all. They had University of California men with them and all the necessary equipment. Tapped all over the mountain and explored thoroughly. I think this proves that only those who are ready for such experiences have them. It's not so much a case of being equipped materially, but being equipped physically.

Fig. 61 - Vintage Mount Shasta Postcard

Personal Experiences

Did We Meet The Elder's of Mt. Shasta?

By Cyril H. Jones

As I write this in 1989, I can't help but remember that it was 4:40 in the afternoon on June 22, 1975, when my wife and I headed up the Everett Memorial Highway that leads from the City of Mount Shasta to the old Shasta Ski Bowl parking lot. We were tired and sticky after a five hour drive through the upper Sacramento Valley in temperatures that were well over the hundred degree mark. We had hoped for cooler weather on the mountain, but it was beginning to appear as though we were in for a hot climb.

About a mile out of town, we encountered two tall, rather thin men, who were walking up the steep road with heavy packs on their backs. Heat waves rose off the road as the afternoon summer sun hammered the asphalt. We never stop for hitch hikers, in fact the men were not hitchhiking, but as we passed I could tell they were laboring under their loads. It was very strange; almost without realizing what I had done, I pulled over to wait for them.

When they caught up to our camper I couldn't believe what I was looking at Two young men of well over six feet were peering in the window with gaunt faces and vibrant eyes of electric blue! My wife and I must have had a strange expression on our faces because we were fascinated by the unusual color of their eyes. Politely, one of the men stepped forward and asked, with an unidentifiable accent, if we had stopped for them. Both were wearing what appeared to be faded Army surplus clothing and were carrying old Army backpacks, but neither one had hiking or climbing boots on; only bare feet in simple leather sandals. Almost at once I became aware of a small chamois pouch that hung from each of their braided leather belts, and it was then I remembered a friend telling me long ago that according to the stories, Lemurians would trade diamonds from soft leather pouches for items from townspeople.

We told them to get into the camper, and then started up the road again. They sat quietly as we wound our way up the road. Then at just about timberline the man who did the talking before put his face up to the boot and asked if I'd stop so they could get out. I must not have believed him, because he had to ask twice. I pulled over, they thanked us and got out, but before they disappeared into the thick manzanita, the one who had done the talking wanted to know where we were going, and if I had built our Aristocrat camper myself... a strange question indeed.

Every school boy has heard stories of the lost continent of Atlantis, but the first time I heard of the lost continent of Lemuria, or Mu, as it is sometimes referred to, I was seventeen years old, and it was a few weeks after I met the stranger in the storm I wrote about in the Spring 1989 issue of UFO UNIVERSE. After telling a friend about my Thanksgiving encounter with the fascinating stranger, he told me about a highly advanced race of tall, fair complected people with eyes the color of Siamese cats eyes who were said to abide deep within the lava caves that honeycombed both Mt. Shasta and Shastina, the crater-ed peak that rises on the north ridge of Mt. Shasta, in Northern California. He said these illusive people were the remnants of a super civilization that all but vanished from the planet some twenty-six thousand years ago after their super continent, Lemuria, had been destroyed and sank into the Pacific Ocean.

He told me that from time-to-time one or two, or even three of these tall thin people had been seen walking through the forests on or near the slopes of the mountain by local inhabitants. He said reports were always the same: they wore flowing white robes and moved through the trees as though they were floating. Upon discovery, they would vanish as though the forest itself was cloaking their presence; protecting their secret. I was told that magnificent crystal bells, so transparent no light reflected from them, stood at the entrance to the lava cave that led down to the great subterranean cities of lletheleme and Yak-tayvia, and the Lemurian's highly advanced civilization.

He said Lemuria's civilization dated back some 78,000 years and lasted in the form of an empire for 52,000 years, reaching heights so great our present civilization would pale by contrast. Government, religion and science reached such perfection as to be far beyond our comprehension.

On the continent of Lemuria there was one language and one government. Education was the cornerstone of the empire's success, and every child's education was compulsory to the age of twenty-one. Then and only then, he or she was eligible to attend citizenship school, and that training lasted for seven additional years. Every citizen was well versed in the laws of the Universe and given thorough training in a profession or trade which resulted in a high degree of cultural prosperity.

It was the Lemurian's belief that the only real purpose of a civilization was to promote the development of advanced egos. They held that without a proper philosophy to guide mankind, there could be no progress. The Lemur-ian understood that Truth (with a capitol "T") was the root of advancement, that a sound, tranquil civilization was the climate, and Man's mind was the fertile soil; together they would give rise to human perfection.

The empire's spiritual and intellectual rise was far more rapid than its technological and industrial development. A compelling need for manual labor that was not educated in Universal Law and the high maxims of citizenry sowed the seeds of annihilation of the Lemurian Empire.

In the end, the Empire became undermined by a corrupt priesthood and a wisdom-lacking work force. Civil war broke out and within a very short time chaos reigned. Interestingly enough, about this same time, the continent was rent by tremendous earthquakes and subterranean explosions until one night the continent collapsed and sank beneath the waters of the Pacific Ocean.

Legend has it that a few good and wise people managed to leave Lemuria just before the great cataclysm, and seek refuge inside the vast lava caves in and around Mt. Shasta where they had set up a stable successor state that has lasted to this day. They keep almost entirely to themselves and view our society as a curiosity.

Well, it all sounded pretty neat to a seventeen year old mind and I thought I'd like to know more, but back in 1954 in a small California town I could only find sketchy verbal information, most of which came from my friend.

Years passed, but I always remembered what little I had been told about the mystic mountain and I was eager to listen to other stories and legends of the place, always trying to add to what I knew. I even made several trips to the mountain, climbing high on its snow covered shoulders looking for Bigfoot, Lemurians, UFOs - and perhaps even the beautiful crystal bells. Adventure was the name of the game and the order of the day.

We spent a restless night in our camper in the vacant parking lot at the end of the road. It was warm and still; not a breath of breeze stirred through our open windows. We could hear trucks changing gears on 1-5 several miles away and over three thousand feet below, and every once-in-a-while we would wonder out loud who the men we helped were, why they wanted out in the middle of nowhere, and what they were doing on the mountain. We couldn't get their penetrating blue eyes out of our minds, and several times we asked each other if they might be of the fabled Lemurian civilization said to be far beneath the mystic mountain we were on. Then we got to speculating about the possibility of them being aliens from another planet, returning to a secret UFO base hidden somewhere inside the mountain; perhaps connected to the Lemurian culture in some way.

By six the next morning we began to climb to the summit. With packs and climbing gear we headed up to Sergeants Ridge with the idea in mind we would make camp at the 11,500 foot level, spend the night and try for the summit the next day.

Home of the Underground Dwellers and Ancient Gods

The winter and spring of 1975 was a drought year in California, making the climb much more difficult than we had expected because there was very little snow on the ground. Mt. Shasta is nothing but a gigantic rock pile, and most of the time we had to pick our way over, around and through rocks of every size. The climb was one of those, three steps forward, one step back affairs that seemed endless.

Ten o'clock found us pitching our tent on a level patch of rocks just below the ridge, and noticing a beautiful lenticular-shaped cloud forming in the deep blue sky over the summit. By the time we had pitched our tent and stowed our gear, the cloud had grown to block out the sun entirely, and within minutes our world had gone from balmy and nice to zero visibility with a twenty-five mile wind. By noon it had started to sleet, and I measured the wind at almost thirty mph.

It was plain to see that we would no doubt be there for quite some time, so we climbed into our sleeping bags and settled down for a nap only to be awakened a short time later by a bright flash of lightning, followed in a few seconds by a tremendous clap of thunder. Things had gone from bad to worse; it had begun to snow!

About mid-afternoon we were seeing the lightning flash and hearing the thunder at the same instant. The tent was taking a terrific beating and we had to keep slapping the sides to lighten the snow loading. Interestingly enough, we felt at peace in our little abode, and for the most part experienced little fear. I don't know why, I mean it was clear we could have been zapped by a lightning bolt at any time, but we rather enjoyed the experience of being that powerless in the presence of raw nature.

Throughout the afternoon and evening the storm gained intensity until several times I thought the aluminum tent poles would snap, and we'd be left with only two thin layers of rip-stop nylon between us and the driving snow. Sounds were about all we had to go on to judge our environment. Tremendous claps of thunder were intense and at quite regular intervals. The screaming wind and the sound of snow pelting against our tent was incessant, punctuated only occasionally by brief periods of an almost eerie silence. As the saying goes, it warn't fit out for man nor beast.

Then at about three in the morning, at the very height of the tempest, we heard the impossible; foot steps crunching through the snow just outside our tent. I don't know which of us heard it first, but I was the one who asked if I were hearing things, or did it sound like foot steps circling our tent in the fresh snow.

With wide eyes, my wife confirmed it sounded like someone - or some thing - was slowly walking around the tent, stopping from time-to-time, and then continuing. We spoke in whispers as we wondered who or what it could be out there in the blizzard. Was it the inscrutable Bigfoot, Lemurians trying to find their way back to the crystal bells, or was it climbers foolishly groping their way back down the mountain in the middle of the night, at the very height of the storm? Not ready to expect other people to be on the move on the mountain in the storm, we were simply too afraid to unzip the fly and look outside. So for several very long minutes the sound of feet crunching in the snow continued as we lay very still in our sleeping bags, straining every nerve in our ears, trying to determine the number of feet and direction of travel. Then, as quickly as it had begun, the sound ceased never to resume.

Unable to sleep for the rest of the night, we lay there pondering what caused the sound, and again got to thinking about the tall men with the very unusual blue eyes we had let out of our camper just below timberline. Who were they, why did they head off through the thick manzanita where there was no trail, and what if any connection did they have with our experience? Were they watching over us; making sure we were safe? In any event, it was one of those unexplainable experiences that poses more questions than it answers, and forever changes the way you look at your world.

It could well be that we met two Elders from Lemuria that day on Mt. Shasta.

Fig. 62 - NASA Rendition of Mount Shasta

Fig. 63 - Ariel View of Mt Shasta summit casting its shadow

Fig. 64 - Model of Bigfoot seen around Shasta

Personal Experiences

Our UFO/Bigfoot Investigation

Some Interesting Exchanges From The Jazma Online Forum

Fig. 65 - The Mount Shasta Bigfoot Investigative Team gathers together as they start their work on the mountain.

Topic author: Silhouet98

Subject: Mt. Shasta UFO/Bigfoot Pre-Investigation

Posted on: 10/05/2007 10:01:30 PM

Message:

HPI Chronicles: The Mount Shasta U FO/Bigfoot/Lemurian/G hosts Pre-Investigation. By Paul Dale Roberts, HPI Ghostwriter, Haunted America Tours Staff Writer

The week before the pre-investigation, I was thinking how our October 6, 2007 Saturday Scouting Investigation went at The Leger and Leonard Lake/Charles Haunting Crime Scenes. It was a success, but I am regretting not stopping at the Argonaut Mine. We drove past it slowly, we looked at it, but we didn't stop to investigate. One of the greatest mining disasters happened at the Argonaut Mine, where many lives were lost. I believe there is plenty of residual haunting activity at this mine location.

Going over my emails, I received this email from Deb Gibble on Mount Shasta:

"One night recently, on Coast to Coast AM, a guy called in and said he was hiking alone in the Trinity Alps area or somewhere up there where he had a good view of Shasta, and he saw not one but two F15's fly INTO the mountain. It's like the mountain opened up and they went in and the door closed, like Aladdin's cave or the Pied Piper or something! The reason he called in is people were speculating where Steve Fossett might be, and the man was suggesting Fossett's plane, too, might have been swallowed up. The phone conversation you had implies to me that, let's call them the 0 club, is monitoring paranormal sites or activities. I don't think it's a bad thing. I'm glad they're curious about the universe, too! Take care. Deb Gibble"

Deb Gibble is referring to this conversation I had from a man who calls himself TR from the OSIR: Here is how it actually went down, from my notes:

On October 5, 2007, Friday, I received a phone call on my cellular phone. The time was about 5:45am. Here is the conversation that took place.

Paul: Hello? (thinking it was my boss).

TR: Hello, you can call me TR, I am with the OSIR.

Paul: OSIR? As in the Office of Scientific Investigation and Research?

TR: Yes. Are you still conducting the pre-investigation at Mt. Shasta?

Paul: Yes, October 13.

TR: Where will you post your story first?

Paul: On the forum at HPI.

TR: Anywhere else? The HPI forum is not an open forum, will you post it at your own site Jazma Online!?

Paul: Yes. TR-. Do you plan to fictionalize the story or are you reporting the story as Truthful?

Paul: Truthful... why?

TR: If you and your team see anything of significance, we may be in contact with you, we may want to talk with you. Are you okay with this?

Paul: Sure.

TR: Thank you.

Paul: Can I contact you while I am at the summit?

TR: No, we will wait for your article, if needed we will contact you.

Paul: Okay.

TR: Thank you, goodbye.

Paul: Goodbye.

As I looked back on my phone, the numbers were 0000 indicating a secure line from the government. I am aware of the 0000 because with a government job I had, I had to deal with the FBI all the time. When the FBI called, it was always 0000. If this is not the OSIR, then it is someone in the government that is curious on our findings. It could even be NORAD for all I know. The interesting thing is ... why would Mt. Shasta have UFO cams on the mountain, if someone isn't really interested. OSIR in the UFO community is rumored to be government funded and some suspect the funds come from the CIA. Dan Ackroyd in the 80s came out with a television called Psi Factor based on the activities of the OSIR.

Here is the official OSIR website: http://www.osironline.org/

'To better understand the OSIR, which for the longest time was a covert agency, which recently went overt and then back to covert status, see this article:

I believe the OSIR website that we now see, which is overt is actually a group of people who have taken on the name OSIR and they are not the real OSIR, but of course this is my opinion. I later learn from paranormal investigator Chris Grissom, that this telephone call could have been hoaxed and the 0 numbers could have been done by telephone spoofing. Rats! I thought I had the real Men in Black after me!

Like Jim Phelps of Mission Impossible's I.M. Force, I am going over the bins, profiles and photos of some of the HPI paranormal investigators and I am amazed at the variety of members we have in HPI with very interesting backgrounds. Holly DeLaughter's ex-father in law is Country Music Hall of Famer Hollis R. 'Red Lane" DeLaughter. Donna Reynolds is a witch of the Sacred Fire Circle and going through her emails, she tells me that I should check out their festivals and write an article, she goes into details to tell me the upcoming festivals they are having, like: Dark Moon Circle on Wednesday, October 10, 2007; Full Moon Circle on 10/26; Wanda's Autumn Bazaar at her shop in Elk Grove on 10/27; an All-Hallow's Eve event at her shop on 10/31; and their

Home of the Underground Dwellers and Ancient Gods

Samhain Celebration on 11/10. Donna at the last minute had to cancel, due to some serious issues she needed to take care of. We do have some interesting 'characters' in HPI.

Now to the pre-investigation at hand. The date is October 13, 2007, Saturday. Roll Call for Paranormal Investigators/ Ufologists/ Cryptozoologists: Paul Dale Roberts, Lead Investigator/Scout, Michele Stump/Researcher, Chris Grissom/Technician, Nicole Rae Pollard, Holly DeLaughter/Psychic, Kelley Tuttle/Guide/Psychic, Bruce Rose berry/Guide, Glennis Roseberry/Guide/Mt. Shasta Historian, Hanako Zeidenberg.

The reason why I gave us all titles of Ufologists and Cryptozoologists, because we all earned our merits for being a Cryptozoologist by tracking Bigfoot and a Ufologist by UFO skywatching this night.

Let's talk about the history of this magic mountain, we all know as Mount Shasta:Mount Shasta was formerly known as Strawberry Valley, Berryvale and Sisson. A long history of mythology surrounds the mountain, including legends of Lemurians, Atlanteans, Secret Commonwealth citizens, dwarfs, fairies, Bigfoot, and space beings who materialize at will. The Indians believed Mt. Shasta was a portal to other dimensions. Bigfoot of course is associated with UFOs and is considered an interdimensional being that can walk into this reality and his own dimensional reality at will. Mt. Shasta is a very special place to say the least-, it represents much more than just a mere mountain. Mt. Shasta can be considered as one of the most sacred places on this planet. The mountain is a mystic power source for this planet. Some people theorize that it is connected to a leyline, similar to Stonehenge in England. It is a focus for angels, spirit-guides, spaceships, masters from the Light Realm, Wicca and the home of the survivors of Ancient Lemuria, which sank under the waves of the Pacific Ocean a little over 12,000 years ago.

The last of the Lemurians and some believe the last of the Atlanteans (of Atlantis) retreated to underground caverns in this sacred mountain. People who have been in the caverns, claim to hear the sound of machinery. In the 1930s, little people with bags of gold would come out of the caverns and trade their gold for goods provided by the farmers.

For those gifted with clairvoyant abilities, Mt. Shasta is embraced in a gigantic, etheric purple pyramid whose capstone reaches far beyond this planet into space, and connects us intergalactically to the Confederation of Planets for this sector of the Milky Way Galaxy. This awesome pyramid is also created as an inverted version of itself, reaching far down to the very core of the Earth. You can call Mt. Shasta the entry point of the Light-Grids of this planet, where most of the energy comes first from the galactic and universal core before it is disseminated to other mountains and into the grids. Most mountaintops, especially tall mountains, are Beacons of Light, feeding the light-grids of this planet. Strange lights and sounds are often seen or heard on the mountain. Lenticular clouds, shadows and outstanding sunsets add to the mystical aura of the mountain. Several tunnels stretch far into the interior of this majestic mountain. People come here to seek out the present-day Lemurians, survivors of the sinking of the continent of Mu. Yes, our Lemurian brothers and sisters are real-, they are well and physically alive, living in the subterranean city of "Telos" beneath Mount Shasta, so legend has it!

The Lemurians, Atlanteans were a highly evolved race of people, that surpass our own living styles with their advanced technology. Many people believe that these ancient civilizations were visited by the gods (extraterrestrials). Prior to the sinking of their continent, fully aware of the eventual destiny of their beloved continent, the ancient Lemurians, using their mastery of energy, crystals, sound and vibrations, hollowed out a vast underground city, with the intention of preserving their culture, their treasures, and their records of ancient Earth's history-, history that has been lost since the sinking of Atlantis. Lemuria was once a vast continent, and larger than North America, connected to parts of California, Oregon, Nevada and Washington. This large continent disappeared overnight into the Pacific Ocean over 12,000 years ago in a vast cataclysm. All inhabitants of the Earth at that time considered Lemuria, the land of Mu, their motherland, and there was much weeping on the Earth when that happened. About 25,000 Lemurians at that time were able to migrate into the interior of Mt. Shasta, the most important of their various administration centers, prior to the sinking of their Motherland. They are still here in tangible, physical, immortal bodies, totally unlimited, living a life of pure Heaven on Earth. American Indians believed that Mt. Shasta was of such immense grandeur, that its existence could only be attributed to the creation of a very "Great Spirit". They also believed that an invisible race of little people, about four feet tall, lived along its slopes as Guardians. These wondrous little people, often referred to as "The Little People of Mt. Shasta", are also kind of physical, but not quite, and they are very often seen visually around the mountain. They are third dimensional beings like humans, but they live on a slightly higher level of the third dimension, such as third and one half level, and they have the ability to make themselves visible and invisible at will. I think I explained enough about the history.

Now let's talk about this pre-investigation to this sacred mountain. 07:30 Hours: Chris Grissom & Michele Stump arrive at my doorstep. We pack up my vehicle 'GhostTracker' and hit 1-5 North towards Redding. We arrive at Starbucks at 1400 Eureka Way for a briefing at 1300 hours. I explain to them the history of Mt. Shasta and the purpose of our investigation. The reason for our investigation is merely to seek the truth. Kelley Tuttle, a resident of Redding, discusses other information about Mt. Shasta to the team and will guide us to the campground, being prepared by Bruce & Glennis Roseberry. Kelley who was very enthusiastic uses white shoe polish and writes on the three vehicles heading to Mt. Shasta 'HPI Paranormal' across the back windows. The MIB won't have a hard time spotting us out. Kelley equips each driver of the three vehicles with walkie-talkies. We convoy up to the campsite with Kelley leading. During the whole stretch everyone is talking on the walkie talkies about this and that in regard to Mount Shasta. I glance down at the book Holly loaned me called 'The Lost Civilization of Lemuria - The Rise and Fall of the World's Oldest Culture by Frank Joseph.'

Michele Stump, our historian/researcher doesn't waste time going through the contents of this book. As we head up the mountain, there was one black government type of vehicle going down the opposite way. The woman in the car, wore dark sunglasses and a suit with black tie. What was odd is I am going up towards the mountain and she is going down the mountain and our eyes connected as we passed. Well, it just seemed odd. After that odd glance with the possible MIB, we chatted more on the walkie talkies and talked about how the weather gods were on my side. The skies were very clear and it was a warm day. There were many naysayers that thought this day would be cloudy and rainy. It rained hard on Friday, but I did a General George S. Patton prayer for good weather and it worked! I also told everyone how I stopped in the small town at Arbuckle and I was waiting forever for this pick-up to move and finally gave up and crossed over. I look back and a Colusa County Sheriff pulled me over. He said I didn't yield. I explained politely the situation and he ran my plates and let me go. Whew! Besides the walkie talkie chatter, I had to listen to Michele and Chris argue about the 49ers and the Cowboys. Michele had her 49er jersey on and Chris had his Cowboy jersey on.

We met up with Bruce and Glennis at Black Bear Restaurant and Bruce and Glennis lead the convoy to the campsite. It was a perfect campsite, we had a clear view of Mount Shasta and the open sky. I went over the equipment that was assigned to everyone. Let's go over it here:

Paul: Listen Up sound enhancer, police band walkie talkie (not used), cell phone, digital camera, binoculars, 2 flashlights, 1 red laser light. Note: laser lights and flashlights are to signal UFOs, some UFO groups use this method to signal UFOs and they in turn signal back. I signaled the Morse Code for 'hello'.

Holly & Nicole: 2 digital cameras, EMF detector, 2 cellphones, 2 Listen Up sound enhancers, 2 laser pen lights, audio digital recorder, video camera, telephoto lens (Cannon & Rebel cameras), dowsing rods, video camera, 2 flashlights. Note: Nicole became a spotter for Bigfoot using binoculars.

Hanoko: digital camera, cell phone, tent, sleeping bag. Note: Hanoko became a spotter for the group surveying the hills with binoculars.

Michele: tent, digital camera, cell phone, binoculars, telescope, night scope.

Glennis: digital camera, cell phone, 2 sets of binoculars, tent.

Chris: flashlight, cell phone.

Kelley: tent, EMF gauge detector, retracting telescope, digital camera, binoculars, digital audio recorder.

As we set up tents, gathered rocks for a makeshift fire site, I looked upon the hillside and saw a long-haired topless woman moving about frantically. I instantly thought, could this be a lovely Nordic alien woman moving about the bushes? I had to go up and investigate. It was actually Nicole, with her long Lady Godiva hair, she threw off her top because she ran into a nest of wasps. She actually got stung 15 times. She was like a champ and after I took out the wasps out of her hair, she continued to assist everyone in gathering firewood.

While we still had daylight, we did a Bigfoot Scouting Mission. Our objective is to gather any Bigfoot hair or dung samples. We were to look for any Bigfoot nesting area and try and locate some Bigfoot footprints in the mud, in which we would have took photos of the footprints and placed Plaster of Paris around the footprint for analysis. The spotters were Nicole & Michele for this scouting mission, both using high-powered binoculars. During this Mission, I was also looking for Angel Hair (associated with UFOs. UFOs are known to deposit Angel Hair that is almost like a spider's web. It disintegrates quickly - no Angel Hair found).

As night fell, everyone shared snacks and beverages. I brought cheese, ham, Ritz crackers, Cheez-its, Pepsi. Kelley treated us to apple streudel pastry. Other members brought a variety of snacks to munch on, as we prepared the telescopes for observation of Mount Shasta and the open night skies. During this night sky watch, we signaled the skies with our laser pen lights and high-powered flashlights. Signaling UFOs was not successful; we did not obtain any signals back. During this UFO investigation, I had Hanoko drive the Ghost Tracker (I was tired of driving) to the local store for necessities for the group. After driving around in the pitch darkness for a good long while, we decided to go back, before we got lost. It's amazing how all of the streets look the same in the deep woods of this Alpine forest. Hanoko was having a good time, this was her very first UFO/Bigfoot investigation and we talked about how we first arrived I threw on some Halloween music 'Thriller by Michael Jackson' and finally some Rick James. When another camping party told us if we can turn down the music, I said to everyone....'oops! That brought me back to reality, I remember we need to do a serious investigation up here', as I turned down the music. Hanoko and I, never did find that store.

We had a couple of mishaps that we now look back at and laugh. I am reminded by this team, that whatever happens in Mt. Shasta stays in Mt. Shasta!

So, I will not disclose those hilarious mishaps.

Most of the group stayed up most of the night, I had a whistle, so in case anyone fell asleep, I was going to blow my whistle and wake up the group if I saw a UFO during 3am to 5am. Guess what? I fell asleep. I was so disappointed in myself that I could not stay up for that long. I literally passed out in my car; it must be that high altitude. This was an exciting pre-investigation and the whole team had felt like family. Michele felt a spiritual connection to this mountain. I was saddened that Michele lost her $900.00 wedding ring at this campsite. She lost it by taking off her gloves. In the morning time, we looked and looked and it was nowhere to be found. I made contact with Shannon 'Ms. Macabre' McCabe, President of H.P.I. and told her about our findings, I placed her on speaker phone as she talked with this group. Unfortunately, we did not capture an alien 'gray' and hogtie it for positive proof that aliens do exist, nor did we gather any dung samples to place on Shannon's doorstep the next day. None of us received an anal probe either. After I told Shannon about my findings... she could only say one thing...'rock and roll!' It was nice sitting around the campfire, telling jokes, talking about the legends of Mt. Shasta. Glennis and Bruce, who frequently visit Mount Shasta, had so many historical insights about this magic mountain. Glennis explained to us how a group of Indians were massacred near and around Mount Shasta and that perhaps there is a lot of residual haunting activity at this location.

I thank the guides, Kelley for leading us to the campsite and Glennis and Bruce for preparing the campsite for us! We could have not done this mission, without their assistance. I thought to myself, since people claim to see Lemurians, dwarfs, aliens and fairies, couldn't all of these creatures be the same thing. They are all described as being small people. Could fairy circles be the equivalent of crop circles or UFO landing sites? Hmmm. The only tall creatures that exist near Mount Shasta are the Nordics which are compared to as angels, because they are tall, pale and have long blonde hair. Then there is Bigfoot, which is supposedly 10 to 12 feet in height. In the morning, as we all were about to head out, Nicole and Holly said they were having breakfast with Glennis and Bruce at the Black Bear Restaurant and were going to drive up the mountain towards the caverns Sunday morning before heading home. We cleaned up the campsite and everyone gave each other a farewell hug and discussed future scouting missions to places like Whiskey Hill in Redding and some other haunted sites. Since I was tired, I let one more person have the honors of driving the Ghost Tracker home. I let Chris drive the Ghost Tracker home as I took a power nap. Chris drove himself home and then I drove Michele back to my house to retrieve her car and she was heading home with a million errands to do. On our way back, we got a call from Hanoko, she left her sleeping bag in my trunk and we were able to pull off the side of the road, where she was waiting for us to get her sleeping bag. Thank goodness for cellular phones! The next time we investigate Mount Shasta will be next summer and we're bringing a bigger team up with us!

Findings:

Special Note: Most UFO sighting activity occurred around 2200 Hours.

Paul: Using binoculars spies a large animal behind a tree. Could be a large deer. I saw a fast moving object (bright light) shoot straight up from the horizon near Mount Shasta and disappear. Many of the team members were able to see the billions of billions of stars in the night skies, the Milky Way, the Big Dipper and satellites moving across the night sky. The night sky was gorgeous.

Kelley: Her psychic abilities causes her to feel dread at a hollow out tree. Later on this evening, she spotted what she thought was a UFO, fast moving object that disappears as fast as it appeared. Object appeared as a star. Her EMF meter went off on its own during the Bigfoot Scouting Mission. Kelley takes some unusual photographs. One photograph there is light emitting from the trees and all of the light points show the number (21), then another similar photo is taken and all of the light sources from the trees show (5%). Very odd photos.

Holly: Feels a presence further up the hill during the Bigfoot Scouting Mission. Special Note: Holly and Nicole on Sunday morning went with Bruce & Glennis Roseberry to Mount Shasta. In one picture there is what appears to be a dark UFO flying over Mount Shasta with 2 strange black lines across the sky. In another picture, there looks like a daytime orb in the sky. Holly & Nicole saw a strange man, not properly clothed for a hiking trip on the mountain slopes, they looked back and he vanished. Holly & Nicole saw trails from one rock to another rock and the trail ends mysteriously.

Hanoko: Spots 2 UFOs in the night skies using binoculars. They moved swiftly in a linear pattern. Both UFOs moved swiftly from point a to point b and vanished. Both UFOs are separate incidents. The erratic behavior of the swift moving star like objects, were different from meteorite movement, they traveled in linear movement, not a falling star movement. Some object pulsated a variety of colors, from blue to orange, to red.

Bruce: Spots one UFO, didn't get full information on his sighting.

Bigfoot Scouting Mission: Scouts: Nicole, Holly, Hanoko, Paul, Kelley, Michele. Headquarters with walkie talkie was Chris Grissom. Three scouts hear strange shrieking cry from their Listen Up devices. Bigfoot is known to make screeching sounds. No dung samples obtained, the closest dung sample was deer dung and I wasn't about to pick that up! One location of our scouting expedition, we discovered no birds chirping, which we thought was unusual. It has been said that if Bigfoot is nearby, birds will stop chirping. Holly feels that there is a presence further up the hill, but we decide to turn back before it gets too dark. We also heard a loud rustling noise, but that could have been a large mammal.

Now as I close this article, I want to mention I received a nice email from Tommy Netzband of the San Francisco Haunted Haight Walking Tour and he thanked us for tagging along on his tour and enjoyed the article I wrote about his tour. It was a pleasure Tommy! If you ever have a chance to take Tommy's Tour, you will see or learn about: The Panhandle Ghost, Buena Vista Park, Golden Gate Park Ghosts, Cole Street Ghost, Grateful Dead House, Hell's Angel Social Club, Trax Bar Ghost aka Dark Shadow Man, The Running Man Ghost. This is a tour, you will enjoy for more information see: www.iiauri-Led iaiglit.com and www.sfghostsociety.oa.,

For more on H.P.I. Haunted and Paranormal Investigations of Northern California and Haunted America Tours, go to the following websites at: www.hpiparanormal.net and www.hauntedamericatours.net

Paul Dale Roberts, HPI Ghostwriter, HAT Staff Writer

Email: JazmaPika@cs.com

www.jazmaonline.com

Paranormal Cellular Hotline: 916 203 7503 (for comments on this story).

Reply author: Silhouet98

Replied on: 10/15/2007 10:47:36 AM

Message:

From Holly DeLaughter & Nicole Rae Pollard, who continued to investigate Mount Shasta on Sunday, October 14, 2007. They were lead up the mountain by Bruce and Glennis Roseberry. This is what Holly's email says:

Hi guys :)

We made it to the end of the road on Mt. Shasta Saturday. What a beautiful day!!! And would you believe it only takes fifteen to twenty minutes to drive as far as you can up there? The gates were open to the summit just past bunny flat.. and for free! Wow! How incredibly beautiful and POWERFUL!!! Oh. My. God. Bruce and Glennis took us to all the points of interest and sacred spots along the way. Between me and Nicole we got around four hundred geo shots to go through! If you need some mouthwatering shots of the top of Shasta I've certainly got them and am online to upload them now.

I got a lot of 'hits' throughout the day and am still trying to process them. But there's no doubt in my mind that's one of the most gorgeous power spots I've ever encountered! We watched a man (strange looking man) start hiking up the summit and he disappeared after about five minutes. I took pictures of him and got quite a few. Also got pictures of what looked to be symbols on top of the mountain (telephoto lens) and am very excited to see if I'm indeed correct. Boy, I sure hope so! That would be soon cool. We also saw a lot of caves, or what appeared to be caves, at and along the top of the mountain.

Okay, I'm chompin' at the bit to see the pix...

Will be in touch, Holly

OH MY GOD! I HAVE SO MUCH COOL xxxx TO SHOW YOU!!! I FOUND TRAILS AT THE TOP OF SHASTA (IN THE SNOW) THAT START IN THE MIDDLE OF NOWHERE -- COMING OUT OF A ROCK AND GOING DOWNHILL TO ANOTHER ROCK -- AND TOTALLY DISAPPEARING!!! PAUL, THERE ARE TONS OF CAVES I'M SUSPICIOUS ABOUT AND AM NOW OFFICIALLY ON A (((SERIOUS))) WORKOUT SCHEDULE TO GET IN SHAPE AND UP SHASTA NEXT SUMMER!!! ME AND NICOLE DECIDED YESTERDAY WE'RE CLIMBING TO THE TOP!

Fig. 66 - King Whitney Glacier on Mount Shasta
Bigfoot and humans are tiny in comparison to the huge features
on this mystical mountain

Fig. 67 - Ride em cowboys (and cowgirls) at the new stagecoach line

Personal Experiences

Strange Potpourri—The Bleu Ocean Story

By Timothy Green Beckley

Bleu Ocean Tells His Tale

One day, when New York session drummer Bleu Ocean was a young boy living on Mount Shasta at about 3,500 feet, he came home from school to see a strange interloper.

"It was around late October," he said, "and I was there with my cousins. Visibility was medium, as it usually is dismal that time of year anyway. In the distance—about 20 feet at the most—we saw what appeared to be a 'hunched man' that seemed to be covered in hair all over his body. I remember he had slightly long arms. The creature, or whatever it was, was walking away from us. We tried to follow him and as we got closer to him we began to see prints in the snow that looked like a large animal's. We felt we might be in danger. We all had bows and arrows, so we stood in one of the tracks until he was out of sight."

Bleu says that when he was in his early teens, "At night we would hear something like wolves or other howling animals' sounds that originated from the middle of the mountain at about 5,500 feet. It was like a surround sound and it was impossible to pinpoint the location.

"As we heard them, we often decided to pursue them. There were five or six of us teenage boys with bows and arrows. Till one day finally we found ourselves very close to the sound. When we looked up, there were these midget-like 'men' who seemed to be walking on all fours but we couldn't say for sure as we were ourselves frightened and paralyzed. They seemed to be like a herd—15 or 20 of them—and beyond them were three to five larger 'men' who stood over seven feet tall with large staffs in their hands and amazingly long beards. They seemed to be coming out from inside Mount Shasta, from some kind of a cave.

"And it seemed to us like these 'midgets' were protecting their 'masters' just like a dog would its owner. These men I will never forget—as Bleu Ocean lives—there was an illumination to their skin, like a fluorescent light was coming out of them. Later on, when I met Tim Beckley and did one of his UFO conferences, I was told by one of the people at the conference that there was a civilization inside the mountain and that I had not dreamed it up. I had never revealed this to anyone for fear of them thinking I was crazy. But thanks to Tim Beckley, I realized there were strange things on this planet and we are not the only ones here.

Visit Bleu's website at www.bleu-ocean.com

Fig. 68 - Native American Bleu Ocean grew up in and around the Mount Shasta forests

From A Website Called "Bigfoot Encounters"

Mount Shasta Herald—September 30, 1976.

"The controversy over whether or not there really is a hairy creature on Mt. Shasta got added fuel when what appeared to be huge footprints were seen in a subsequent search of the area.

"Mr. Larry More of Mount Shasta went to the scene with his camera two days after a timber faller, Virgil Larson, reported seeing a huge 'non-human' creature with long black hair in the woods south of Cascade Gulch on September 3rd.

"More, Larson, some other loggers, and a Walnut Creek man who was sitting on a rock waiting for a look at the creature, hiked around the area two days later and spotted what appeared to be two footprints, 16 inches long, indented in the dirt.

"The footprints were there, More said, 'But I couldn't say how old they were.'

"Another logger, who wouldn't identify himself, was reported to have seen the creature two days later at Ponto Park east of McCloud, but the sighting was not verified. Mr. More said what appeared to be blood found at the scene where the creature was sighted on Mt. Shasta by Larson was a common condition found all over the woods on peeled dry limbs."

Submitted by Eric Hammond

The tracks were found at the 8000 foot level. I met two gentlemen who said they had seen a Bigfoot while drinking beer in the Bunny Flats Campground. They said the Bigfoot had come out of the forest knocking off a branch at the nine foot level.

The Bigfoot allegedly gave them a crystal and went back into the woods. I never heard of any evidence but they would tell you the story if you would give them beer.

Charlie Tom, a medicine man, taught us a Bigfoot song. He said if you were in trouble in the woods to sing the song and Bigfoot would help you.

From "The Hollow Earth Insider," Dennis Crenshaw
The People Who Live Under Mount Shasta

Just south of the Oregon-California border a majestic peak holds its secrets. Mt. Shasta, at 14,380 feet, dominates the bright California sky, and as legend has it is home of the descendants of the Lost Continent of Lemuria, who live in an underground city. Locals along the trails and roads of this remote, serene area sometimes see strange robed "elders." One such encounter was described by Cyril H. Jones in the May 1990 "UFO Universe."

As he and his wife were driving along the Everett Memorial highway out of the City of Mount Shasta towards the mysterious mountains, they passed two tall, thin men with heavy backpacks on their backs, walking up the steep road. For some unexplained reason, Mr. Jones stopped his camper and let them catch up. Mr. Jones described the meeting:

"Two young men of well over six feet tall were peering in the window with gaunt faces and vibrant eyes of electric blue! My wife and I must have had a strange expression on our faces because we were fascinated by the unusual color of their eyes. Politely, one of the men stepped forward and asked, with an unidentifiable accent, if we had stopped for them." The two men asked to be dropped at the timberline then climbed into the back of his camper.

As they disappeared into the forest, the Jones' noticed the pair were wearing simple leather sandals, unusual footwear for the area.

The next morning, after climbing to the 11,500 foot level, the Jones' pitched their tent. By the time their camp was squared away, a cloud had started to shroud the mountain, blocking the sun. Within minutes, "it had gone from balmy and nice to zero visibility with a twenty-five mile wind." As the day continued, the weather went from bad to worst. Thunder, lightning and driving snow. Mr. Jones described what happened next:

"Then, at about three in the morning, at the very height of the tempest, we heard the impossible: footsteps crunching through the snow outside our tent. With wide eyes, my wife confirmed that it sounded like someone—or some thing—was slowly walking around the tent, stopping from time to time and then continuing on."

The next morning the storm was over. The Jones' made a careful examination of the area around their campsite, but they found nothing.

Had the Jones' nocturnal visitor been one of the elusive animals known as Bigfoot? Or had the two strange men of the day before braved the storm to look over the Jones', repaying the favor of the ride up the mountain by becoming their guardian angels during the raging storm? Had the Jones' met two "elders" from Lemuria? We'll never know. But one thing we do know. The Jones' are certain that during the night their camp above the tree line on the mysterious Mt. Shasta had been visited by someone . . . or something.

From "The New York Times," August 16, 1873
The Creation: According To The Modocs

Mr. Joaquin Miller, in his book entitled "Life Among the Modocs," has given some picturesque sketches of Indian life and traditions. Among much other interesting matter, he tells us that the idea of the creation of the world as it was entertained by the Modocs, now verging on extinction in accordance with the demands of modern civilization, was this: The Great Spirit made Mount Shasta first of all. He pushed down snow and ice from the skies through a hole which he made in the blue heavens by turning a stone round and round, till he made this great mountain; then he stepped out of the clouds onto the mountaintop, and descended and planted the trees all around by putting his finger on the ground. The sun melted the snow, and the water ran down and nurtured the trees and the rivers.

After that, he made the fish for the rivers out of the small end of his staff. He made the birds by blowing some leaves which he took up from the ground among the trees. After that, he made the beasts out of the remainder of his stick, but he made the grizzly bear out of the big end, and made him master over all the others.

Having done that, the Great Spirit converted Mount Shasta into a wigwam, and its volcanic eruptions are the outcome of the fire that he lights in the center of the mountain. The development of man was a later occurrence. The daughter of the Great Spirit, venturing too far, got astray and fell into the power of the grizzly bears, and she was forced to marry one of them, and the red men were the fruit of the marriage. These red men were taken under the protection of the Great Spirit; but the grizzlies were punished by being compelled to walk on four feet, whereas before they had walked on two. To this day, the grizzly bear is never slain by the red men, who recognize in him a sort of kinsman.

We must quote one short anecdote from this book: "I had a pocket Bible with me once. I was young, enthusiastic, and anxious to do a little missionary business on my own responsibility. I showed it to the chief, and undertook to tell him what it was.

"It is the promise of God to man," I said. "His written promise to us that if we do as he has commanded us to do, we shall live and be happy forever when we die."

He took it in his hand, upside down, and looked at the outside and inside very attentively.

"Promises? Is it a treaty?"

"Well, it is a treaty perhaps; at least it is a promise, and he wrote it."

"Did it take all of this to say that? I do not like long treaties on paper. They are so easy to break. The Indian does not want his God to sign a paper. He is not afraid to trust his God."

"But the promises?" I urged.

He pointed to the new leaves of the trees, the spears that were bursting through the ground, handed me the book quietly and said no more.

On Mr. Miller's showing, Christians might learn a great deal of religion from the Modoc Indians.

--"New York Times" article found and submitted by Tim Cridland.

**Fig. 69 - Merrick Rees Hamer (Phylos) and Producer Poke Runyan
At the Sacred Grove on Mount Shasta**

Personal Experiences

An Unsurpassed Visionary Experience
By Poke Runyon

Author, publisher, movie producer . . . Poke Runyon keeps himself busy walking that thin line between reality and an alternative only a few know about. Poke has seen Mount Shasta at its best and its worst. He's spent a lot of time there recently, making his opus "Beyond Lumeria—The Shaver Mystery and the Secrets of Mount Shasta." Running over 90 minutes, this feature was shot admittedly on a "tight budget," yet its meaning and purpose is well thought out. Critics have called it a "dramatic feature film based on accounts that many believe are true." It was photographed entirely at Mount Shasta and in the nearby lava caverns as well as in the lost Lemurian city of Nan Madol. This chapter, written by Poke himself, will take the reader behind the scenes of a world kept hidden from most—2012 and Planet X, the Dero Death Rays, and the darkest secrets of the cavern world inside Mount Shasta and the land of Lemuria.

In July of 2005 I made my first visit to California's famous Mt. Shasta. To reach Shasta by air from Southern California I had to fly to Phoenix, Arizona and then on to Medford, Oregon. There I rented an SUV and drove nearly a hundred miles down through the Cascade Mountains into Northern California. This is a beautiful scenic drive highlighted by the first sight of awesome, distant Mt. Shasta rising in solitary, snow-capped grandeur beyond the vast expanse of lava fields that extend to the foothills of the Cascades on the Oregon border.

It was said that in the old days American Indians could walk underground all the way from Mt. Shasta to Oregon through the labyrinth of caverns under the badlands north of the Sacred Mountain.

I had come to this remote wilderness to scout locations up on the mountain itself and down in the nearby caverns for a feature film we were shooting called *Beyond Lemuria*. This was to be a mystical science-fiction drama based on the original and most noteworthy of Mt. Shasta's mystic avatars, Phylos of Atlantis. Phylos was first revealed by Frederick Spencer Oliver in his 1895 occult classic *A Dweller on Two Planets*. As a counterpoint to the transcendental beauty and inspiration of the Sacred Mountain, the lava caverns just north of Shasta would provide us with the venue for the dark side of our cinematic adventure: the evil

Home of the Underground Dwellers and Ancient Gods

"Deros" from Richard S. Shaver's notorious 'true' accounts of demented Lemurian subterranean dwellers.

In the town of Mt. Shasta I would link up with Ed Fitch, a long time friend and collaborator. Ed had grown up in the Mt. Shasta area and knew the country well. He was an outdoorsman and an avid spelunker. We shared a youthful fascination with "The Shaver Mystery" tales in the old pulp magazine *Amazing Stories*. Ed plays the part of a sinister government agent in our film.

I checked in to a local motel. Ed was running late for our meeting and I had several hours of daylight left so I decided to drive as far up the mountain as I could. Shasta is 14,000 feet high but there is a very good road, the Everitt Parkway that takes you all the way to the timberline from where you can hike up through patches of snow almost to the edges of the glaciers. The scene is a broad sweep of stark, awesome beauty. White snow, black crags, red rocks, gnarled pines and luminous green moss. It sparkles with a crystalline, otherworldliness; clean, sharp and brilliant like a scene from an Abraham Merritt fantasy.

I parked on the highest level below the summit; formerly the location of a ski lodge that had burned down years ago. This was the southwest face of the mountain, just below Green Butte. A thousand yards up the slope, at an elevation of 9,000 feet, was a ridge with a small grove of trees. It seemed to beckon to me. Even though it was getting late in the afternoon I felt compelled to explore the site.

Once I had reached the grove I knew that this was indeed the place where our Phylos would bring his students for meditation in the film. On the flat toward the summit there was not one but two American Indian medicine wheels carefully marked out with stones. In Native American lore Mt. Shasta was where spirits of the dead ascended to the Milky Way; the celestial River of Souls.

I sat down on a boulder in the grove and looked up at the stark, jagged summit of the Sacred Mountain. Time stood still. My mind became calm and totally receptive...

Before long I sensed the presence of someone nearby to my left. Without moving my head I glanced out to the corner of my eye and saw a gray-robed figure sitting on a rock next to me. He was an Oriental of indeterminate age with a large baldhead and a long drooping white moustache. When I turned my head toward him he vanished.

This inspired me to get into an asana and do some serious yoga. I brought my consciousness up to the heart chakra (Tiphareth in Hermetic yoga) and then invoked the Spirit of the Mountain.

A voice whispered deep in my mind: "Not yet."

Somewhat sadly I decided it was time to leave for that day – as indeed it was for the Sun was sinking below distant peaks to the west---But I knew I must return...

The next day Ed Fitch and his two sons, accompanied by a beautiful young lady and another young adventurer, arrived in town. They were well equipped for a spelunking expedition. We provisioned at a local market and headed for the caverns beneath Mt. Shasta's desolate northern lava fields.

This whole vast area to the north of the looming Shasta summit is a waste land of jagged lava rocks, scrub brush and stunted, gnarled trees. Tolkien's Mordor comes to mind, or perhaps one of H. P. Lovecraft's haunted wastelands – a fitting place for a labyrinth of Dero-haunted caves---and the Indians believed that the caverns were inhabited by "giant creatures who squeezed their victims to death."

The first cavern we explored was called Barnum's cave. It was interesting, even challenging, but not suitable for our film. We headed up the country road to our main destination: Pluto's Cave.

The Pluto's Cave complex is unique in some respects. The roof has fallen in several places forming what are called "skylights" which provide natural illumination to the galleries. This feature was ideal for filming and would save us much time, trouble and expense in lightning equipment. Pluto is not a tourist attraction and is actually rather difficult to find. Perhaps this is intentional because the cave is deceptive. The first three naturally lighted sections are not difficult for spelunkers, but when you enter the total darkness at the far end of the complex you could be heading into serious trouble. Nobody knows how far back the cave goes. When you come to that high, vaulted archway framing an endless, stygian darkness, you recall Dante's warning: "Abandon hope all ye who enter here!"

Geologically Pluto is 200,000 years old. The section we called "Satan's Cathedral" was created by a huge lava bubble that formed a nearly perfect vaulted dome sixty feet high; a fitting place for our cinematic villains to perform a satanic ritual and summon a Dero.

Pluto's Cave is obviously the location where the old Shasta prospector J. C. Brown had discovered an underground chamber, decorated with mysterious hieroglyphics and filled with golden treasure, back in 1904. We use a representation of J. C. Brown's treasure map showing a cross section of Pluto's Cave in Beyond Lemuria.

Following our Pluto reconnaissance, Ed Fitch and his spelunking team took off for another location, leaving me time to return to the Sacred Mountain before sundown. As I drove up Everitt Parkway toward Panther Meadows the glowing green moss on the trunks of the tall pine trees along the roadside suddenly jogged my memory -- I had had a vivid dream of traveling this very same road only a few weeks before! This realization triggered an altered state of consciousness. The world began to shimmer with a strange light. It was as if I had entered another dimension.

I knew with a certainty that I was on the verge of a mystic revelation.

I parked at Ski Bowl as before. The parking area was deserted. I trekked up the slope in a steady pace, still in my altered state, but totally aware of and fully connected to my surroundings, as if I was a part of the landscape, a part of the Mountain.

I found the same spot up in the grove and took my asana. After an invoking pentagram ritual I performed pranayama and the mudrahs that bring down celestial light. This time I raised my consciousness up to Chesed (Third eye and cosmic consciousness in Hermetic yoga) and then opened my eyes to contemplate the summit. The sun was still bright in the late afternoon sky but clouds were forming. Once again I invoked the Spirit of the Mountain --- and this time it came!

The spirit seemed to be male (although the Mountain Herself is female). He used my voice and I found myself speaking softly aloud, as I would if channeling an angel in a magical operation. Through me the spirit said:

"My name is (withheld by the author) but I will answer to any honorable name you choose to give me. As you are aware, each sphere of the Tree of Life contains all of the other spheres within itself. Here, on this day, you have attained Kether of Malkuth. You have achieved this level of understanding by climbing the Holy Mountain in a spiritual state of mind, and thus becoming one with the Mountain. You know that a human being is a miniature of the greater universe. You have all the spheres and the planets within yourself, but you are the child of Mother Earth. She is the most potent planetary presence within you---so when you ascend the Holy Mountain, where Earth reaches up to Heaven, you are at the summit of your mystic consciousness. Here you will meet your ancestors and review your previous incarnations. Do not take these visions to be illusions. They are more real than the shadow world of your everyday affairs. Here you will learn the secrets of ages long gone by.

You can indeed find the hidden entrance to an ancient temple of wisdom high on this Sacred Mountain, because that Temple has always existed in your deepest memory. You become one with the Mountain and within the Mountain is the Secret Temple. This is the Great Arcanum of Mt. Shasta....."

And at that moment the Sun went behind a cloud. It was as if a light switch had been turned off. The Spirit was gone. My altered state quickly dissipated and I was once again in the so-called "real" world. I reluctantly performed a banishing pentagram and then trekked down the mountain to my vehicle. Yes, I had returned to the real world, but I was not the same person I had been before the experience. Now I shared with Frederick Spencer Oliver, Guy Ballard and others who had climbed the Holy Mountain a profound experience. I had received Mt. Shasta's initiation.

In the months to come I recovered more significant memories of previous lifetimes and experiences than at any time in my thirty nine years as a practitioner and teacher of Hermetic magick. I attempted to dramatize the essence of my Mt. Shasta experience in the revelations of the Avatars depicted in our film *Beyond Lemuria*. In this regard we were fortunate in having the noted author and magical teacher Lon Milo DuQuette portray the sage Hermes Trismegistus. Hermes makes a visionary appearance above the Holy Mountain and delivers the ultimate secret knowledge at the climax of our film.

Mt. Shasta is indeed America's Holy Mountain and I will treasure my mystic experience on her slopes for many lifetimes to come.

Poke Runyon

(Magister Thabion)

Writer-Producer,
Beyond Lemuria,
The Shaver Mystery and the Secrets of Mt. Shasta

Fig. 70 - Pluto's Cave North of Mount Shasta

Fig. 71 - Master Phylos Teaches on Mount Shasta

Fig. 72 - Master Phylos on the slopes of Mount Shasta

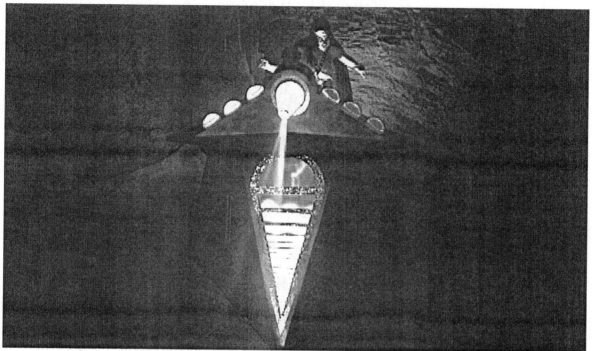

Fig. 73 - Dero Elder Mech Ray Projector

Fig. 74 - Master Phylos at Mount Shasta

Fig. 75 - Poke Runyon as Atlantean High Priest

Fig. 76 - Isabela Shahira as the Lemurian High Priestess

Personal Experiences

Return of The Morning Star

By Dana Howard

*According to the website **UFO Digest,** "There aren't as many female contactees of the Golden Age of UFOs as there are male, but there are a few. One was Dana Howard, who wrote about her encounters in **My Flight To Venus, Diane: She Came From Venus, Over the Threshold** and **Vesta, the Earthborn Venusian** as well as others. As we can see Dana was a prolific writer!" It is from her perspective as a 1950s contactee that Dana presents the following.*

The story of Mount Shasta has been told and re-told but to this day it still remains the unsolved enigma of the north-west United States. Perhaps even this riddle can now be solved through the coming of the flying saucers. It is not only possible, but probable that Mount Shasta and other highly consecrated points on our globe are the actual conditioning stations for visitors from outer space. It would seem like sound reasoning logic to assume that voyagers from other planets upon first coming into our earth's orbit would have to be conditioned to our atmosphere. They would need to adapt themselves not only physically, but they would need to accommodate themselves to our thought processes. We earthlings learn to conform even in small ways (and in fact, since the human race is the most "adaptable" life-form on this planet, then why not on other planets as well? - Ed.). Interplanetary visitors would necessarily have to harmonize and fit into the lowered vibration of our earth...

While this is extraneous to average intelligent thinking, we must realize we are living today in the greatest era the human race on this planet has ever known. This takes us out of the bounds of the usual and forces us to round new corners. It brings us ever closer to events that make the stars stand still. However, once we are irrefutably convinced these so-called flying saucers are coming from outer space, we will then be able to accept the star-standing-still events without quibble or question.

This is where the hitherto unsolved mystery of Mount Shasta might shed some small measure of light over the broad scope of doubt. For several hundred years past, the tall, pine-treed cliffs of Mount Shasta have held inviolate a secret believed by many to embrace a long-dead tradition. There are geologists and other men of science who proclaim it the oldest land on earth--a consecrated plot cut off from that mythical continent known as Lemuria (also referred to by many other names, including "ELAM", "MU", "PAN", and others - Ed.). It is believed by many that in some miraculous way this plot of earth escaped the cataclysms of long ago.

For many years Mount Shasta has been the object of serious investigations not only by the few steeped in occult lore and traditional romanticism, but by scientists, the press, educators and just good neighbors living in the valleys beneath the high peaks. Untold numbers have given evidence that on occasions too numerous to mention they have seen streams of blue-white light emanating from the Shasta heights. These lights appeared long before Thomas Edison gave us the electric light and it is said they often extended a beam as far south as the San Francisco Bay...

**Fig. 77 - One of the few female contactees, Dana Howard
promotes her book at Giant Rock UFO convention**

Researchers assert the State of California is posited on very old land. In fact it has often been called "the cradle of humanity" and not a few believe it to be the actual site of that fabulous Garden of Eden. Relics have been unearthed from one end of the state to the other that take us back into an almost extinct past.

California's rare old trees, the Sequoia and Redwoods, to say nothing of an unusual specimen of Frankincense Tree found growing a few short years ago in the Borrego Desert. Enough substantiating facts can be gathered together to bear evidence that California might well have been the scene of the original paradise. (Editors Note: If we are to believe that, as many have suggested, the legendary continent of Lemuria was in fact the "cradle" of mankind's first great civilizations, or "Adamic Man," then it may well have had some connection to the "Garden of Eden" legend in the Bible, as well as the "Deluge" legends which appear not only in the Bible, but among the legends of civilizations and native inhabitants throughout the entire world. If the Western United States is the last remnant of that sunken continent, then the area surrounding Mt. Shasta just may be one of the oldest places on earth - Ed.)

Mount Shasta is part of California's Noahian soil. This would make the peak of Mount Shasta the cone of an antediluvian volcano (incidentally, some tribes of north California Indians have a legend which states that men and animals were saved from the "Great Flood" by taking refuge on the summit of Mt. Shasta, which was not entirely covered by the flood - Ed.). At the foot of the mountain buried deep in the rocks searchers have found more than twelve hundred feet of hieroglyphics that to this day have not been deciphered. These rock writings are said to be totally different from anything known to the long red line of American Indians.

In recent years, many persons living in the lower areas declare that in days gone by they often saw men of strange appearance in their midst. They have been described as tall and stately with an aura of maturity and wisdom about them that set them apart from other men.

The neighbors report blue-white lights glowing through the tall pine trees. For a time these beams of light created considerable excitement in press circles.

In fact they were almost as provocative as flying saucers. Fabulous yarns have been spun about them--how, when the wind blew in a certain direction they often heard strains of weird music and loud chants. Many of these same persons have gone on record as stating they have also seen fantastic sky ships floating in the skies around Mount Shasta. They have been described as "peculiar silver-like vessels" that appeared and disappeared. Occasionally one of these ships flew out over the Pacific Ocean. They have been seen by seamen all the way from the California coast line to the Aleutian Islands. And again, investigators by the score have been turned back from their investigative treks by some powerful invisible ray, always encountered at a given point in the high mountain climb.

It would seem within the scope of possibility that Mount Shasta and other pristinely clear points on our globe would be the conditioning areas for visitors from other planets, if in fact they are calling on us. While we may look upon them as a superior people, they are still human. Any foreigner coming into our country and land would have to accommodate to living conditions and the language. They too would have to do likewise.

All of this poses another question... were these strange-appearing men so often seen below the cliffs of Mount Shasta actually Venusians? Has Mount Shasta been one of their bases for more years than we know anything about?...

In 1930, shortly before the passing of that grand Old Indian Chief, Francisco Potentio, your author interviewed him in the hope of discovering something new about the mystery of Mount Shasta. Chief Potentio, founder of the fabulous village of Palm Springs, and one of the surviving remnants of the old Cahuilla Tribe was then one hundred and eight years old. From him I learned about the silvery ships that came and went from the highest point of the mountain.

"Sky ships come from Morning Star," the old man said, pointing to the Planet Venus.

Again, if these strange people were in reality the last surviving sparks from a long lost continent now sunk beneath the waves, would they disappear for years at a time? Today one hears nothing about weird music emanating from the Shasta Peaks, nor is there any mention of the odd-looking men seen a few years ago around Weed, California located in the valley below. If they are still there hidden in the deep-recesses of the mountain why do we no longer hear about them? Why have they gone into seclusion?

Then there is another point of view. If these people are in fact the last survivors of the Lemurians,who can say how much or how little Lemurian blood flows in our own veins? During their long sojourn on this continent it is possible many of them deserted the little band and traveled into the valleys. It is even conceivable they might be commingled with the Red Ilan of that day. When the Pilgrim Fathers landed on our shores they were met by a highly evolved and friendly race of Indians. Perhaps they were the sons of the seeds left over from The Morning Star...

Today we are bending our efforts in many directions in an effort to solve our world problems. If our issues are too difficult for us to solve alone it is logical to believe a superior order of life would be sent to help us. It is hard for most of us to realize that the very fabric of our earth's civilization is threatened. When we scoff and jeer at something we do not understand we are only holding back the hands of the clock. In the past our own stubborn fixations have prevented us from looking into the far horizons. Today the whole world is space-minded. We are beginning to realize we are all part of the same universal pattern. Whatever we are capable of "thinking" we can become proficient in DOING. Whether we are aware of it or not we are ably equipped with invisible extension cords with which to make a definite tie with all the domains of existence.

If other planetary beings have come to endow us with new strength and a resurgence of faith it is not necessary that we wear some badge of identification. As strangers coming into our earth's orbit they would naturally exchange the robes of their sojourn for the robes of earth. While they might be instantly teleported to our planet unless they had been here before they would have the same adjustments to make as the newcomers. If they intended to remain for any lengthy stay they would have to adjust to our lowered vibrations. This might require years, hence they would need conditioning bases of the nature of Mount Shasta.

Let us not discredit that which we have not learned to understand. Perhaps the message they have to bring us--is the very message for which we have been waiting these last two thousand years.

Fig. 78 - 'Mt. Shasta by Night' by William Seltzer Rice (1873-1963).

Fig. 79 - Rocket Ship? No- the Geodetic Survey Signal USGS

Fig. 80 - Snowcam Picture of Shasta on April 1, 2008

About Timothy Green Beckley

Tim Beckley has had so many careers that even his own girlfriend doesn't know what he does for a living . . .

Fig. 81 - Timothy Green Beckley- Mr. UFO

Timothy Green Beckley has been described as the Hunter S. Thompson of Ufology by the editor of "UFO Magazine," Nancy Birnes.

From his early childhood, Tim's life has more or less revolved around the paranormal. The house he was raised in was thought to be haunted. Tim experienced out-of-body-experiences at age six, and saw his first of three UFOs when he was but ten.

Tim grew up listening to the only all night talk show in the country that revolved around the strange and unexplained. Long John Nebel's guests included the early UFO contactees who claimed to have visited other planets and built time machines in the desert. Tim was fascinated by everything that went bump in the night—or even in the daylight for that matter. Years later, Tim was to appear on Long John's show numerous times, and over the years has been a frequent guest on hundreds of programs which have come and gone just like ghosts in the night.

Tim started his career as a writer early on. At age 14, he purchased a mimeograph machine and started putting out the "Interplanetary News Service Report." Over the years he has written over 25 books on everything from rock music to the secret MJ-12 papers. He has been a stringer for the national tabloids such as the "Enquirer" and editor of over 30 different magazines (most of which never lasted more than a couple of issues). His longest running effort was the newsstand publication "UFO Universe," which ran for 11 years. Today he is the president of Inner Light/Global Communications and editor of "The Conspiracy Journal" and "The Bizarre Bazaar."

He is one of the few Americans ever to be invited to speak before closed-door meetings on UFOs presided over by the late Earl of Clancarty at the House of Lords in England.

Tim's books include:

Our Alien Planet—This Eerie Earth

Strange Encounters

John Lennon—We Knew You

Secret Prophecy of Fatima Revealed

Subterranean Worlds Inside Earth

Timothy Green Beckley's Strange Saga

UFOs Among The Stars

Tim is also a movie and documentary filmmaker. During the heyday of double features and Times Square grindhouses, he worked as a movie critic as well as a publicist for several small companies. His recent efforts include "Skin-Eating Jungle Vampires" and "Blood Sucking Vampire Freaks."

Fig. 82 - Early Settlers on Mount Shasta

Fig. 83 - Lake Tule in View of Mount Shasta

Fig. 84 - The view of the Leonids with Mt. Shasta as a backdrop - J. Flinn NASA

Fig. 85 - Mount Shasta with Indians and TeePees. Steel engraving by E.P. Brandard, 1873

Fig. 86 - Mount Shasta from Shasta Lake

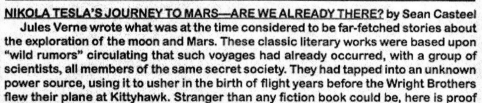

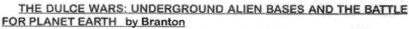

Home of the Underground Dwellers and Ancient Gods
Research and Books on the Inner Earth Mysteries and Related Materials

The Smoky Gods and Other Inner Earth Mysteries
by Olaf Johnson, with Ray Palmer and Shurula
....$15.00

Etidorhpa - Journey to Another Land
"Official Edition"
.... $25.00

Subterranean Worlds Inside Earth
by Timothy Green Beckley
Explorers the Shaver Mystery
....$15.00

Richard Shaver and the Reality of The Inner Earth
by Tim Swartz
....$22.00

The Secret World
Rare hardcover classic with Ray Palmer and
Richard Shaver (featuring his rock book paintings)
....$32.00

Messages From the Hollow Earth
by Dianne Robbins
....$19.95

Telos : The Call Goes Out from the
Hollow Earth and the Underground Cities
by Dianne Robbins
....$18.95

The Phantom of the Poles
By William Reed
....$16.95

Lost Worlds and Underground Mysteries
of the Far East by M. Paul Dare
....$18.00

The Arctic Home In The Vedas
by Lokamanya Bal Gangadhar Tilak
....$23.95

Quest for the Inner Earth
By Dorothy Leon
....$17.95

Twilight: Hidden Chambers Beneath The Earth
by T. Lobsang Rampa
....$22.00

A Dweller On Two Planets
by Phylos the Thibetan
....$19.95

Incredible Cities of the Inner Earth
by David H. Lewis
....$21.95

Mysteries of the Pyramid
by David H. Lewis
....$21.95

Admiral Byrd's Secret Journey Beyond the Poles
by Tim R. Swartz
....$22.00

Caverns, Cauldrons, & Concealed Creatures
Expanded 2nd Edition! By Michael Mott
....$29.95

Finding Lost Atlantis Inside the Hollow Earth
Rare Reprint by Brinsley Le Poer Trench
....$22.00

Missing Diary of Admiral Richard E. Byrd
Lost for years, now in print!
....$15.00

Coming Soon:
Rare reprint of the Hidden World
Long defunct quarterly book issues by
Ray Palmer and containing controversial material
on inner earth, in particular Shaver Mystery.

Order From:
Global Communications, Box 753-TGS, New Brunswick, NJ 08903
MRUFO8@hotmail.com -
Order hot line - 732 602-3407
add $5.00 for shipping